UK Latest Deluxe Edition Ninja Foodi Dual Zone Digital Air Fryer Cookbook

2333 Days Ninja Foodi Dual Zone Digital Air Fryer Recipes Take your culinary creations to the next level.

Mary J. Coles

CONTENTS

Poultry Recipes 35

Recipe Index 103

Introducing the Ninja Foodi Dual Zone Digital Air Fryer

In the world of kitchen appliances, innovation meets convenience with the Ninja Foodi Dual Zone Digital Air Fryer. This state-of-the-art device redefines the art of cooking by combining the functionality of an air fryer with the flexibility of a dual-zone cooking system, providing users with unparalleled control and efficiency in their culinary endeavors.

Advantages of the Ninja Foodi Dual Zone Digital Air Fryer:

Dual-Zone Cooking: One of the standout features of this air fryer is its ability to cook two different foods simultaneously at different temperatures and durations, thanks to its independent cooking zones. This means you can prepare an entire meal at once, saving time and effort in the kitchen.

Large Capacity: With a spacious cooking basket, the Ninja Foodi Dual Zone Digital Air Fryer can accommodate large batches of food, making it ideal for families or gatherings. Whether you're frying up crispy chicken wings or roasting vegetables, there's plenty of room to satisfy everyone's appetite.

Precise Temperature Control: Equipped with a digital control panel, this air fryer allows for precise temperature adjustments, ensuring consistent results with every use. From crispy fries to tender meats, you can achieve the perfect texture and flavor without any guesswork.

Versatile Cooking Functions: Beyond air frying, this appliance offers a range of cooking functions, including roasting, baking, reheating, and dehydrating. Its versatility makes it a valuable addition to any kitchen, allowing you to explore a variety of recipes and cooking techniques.

Healthier Cooking: By using little to no oil, the Ninja Foodi Dual Zone Digital Air Fryer enables you to enjoy your favorite fried foods with significantly less fat and calories. It's a healthier alternative to traditional frying methods, without sacrificing taste or texture.

Tips for Using the Ninja Foodi Dual Zone Digital Air Fryer:

Preheat for Optimal Results: To ensure even cooking and crispy textures, always preheat the air fryer before adding your food. This helps to create a hot and consistent cooking environment from the start.

Rotate and Flip: For evenly cooked results, rotate and flip your food halfway through the cooking process. This allows for uniform browning and crisping on all sides, especially when preparing larger quantities or thicker cuts of meat.

Avoid Overcrowding: While the air fryer has a generous capacity, it's essential not to overcrowd the cooking basket. Leave some space between food items to allow hot air to circulate freely, promoting proper cooking and crisping.

Experiment with Seasonings: Don't be afraid to get creative with seasonings and marinades to elevate the flavor of your dishes. Whether it's a simple sprinkle of salt and pepper or a blend of herbs and spices, seasonings can take your air-fried creations to the next level.

Cleaning and Maintenance:

Regular Cleaning: After each use, allow the air fryer to cool completely before cleaning. Remove the cooking basket and tray and wash them with warm, soapy water. Wipe down the interior and exterior of the unit with a damp cloth to remove any food residue or grease.

Dishwasher Safe Parts: For added convenience, most parts of the Ninja Foodi Dual Zone Digital Air Fryer are dishwasher safe, including the cooking basket, tray, and crisper plate. Simply place them in the dishwasher for easy cleanup.

Deep Cleaning: Periodically, it's essential to perform a deep clean of the air fryer to remove built-up grease or residue. Refer to the manufacturer's instructions for detailed guidance on disassembling and cleaning the unit thoroughly.

In conclusion, the Ninja Foodi Dual Zone Digital Air Fryer revolutionizes home cooking with its dual-zone cooking system, precise temperature control, and versatile functionality. Whether you're a novice cook or a seasoned chef, this appliance offers endless possibilities for delicious and healthier meals, all with the added convenience of easy cleanup and maintenance.

Breakfast Recipes
Sweet Potato Hash

Servings: 4
Cooking Time: 15 Minutes
Ingredients:

- 3 sweet potatoes, peel & cut into ½-inch pieces
- ½ tsp cinnamon
- 2 tbsp olive oil
- 1 bell pepper, cut into ½-inch pieces
- ½ tsp dried thyme
- ½ tsp nutmeg
- 1 medium onion, cut into ½-inch pieces
- Pepper
- Salt

Directions:

1. In a bowl, toss sweet potatoes with the remaining ingredients.
2. Insert a crisper plate in Ninja Foodi air fryer baskets.
3. Add potato mixture in both baskets.
4. Select zone 1 then select "air fry" mode and set the temperature to 355 degrees F for 15 minutes. Press "match" to match zone 2 settings to zone 1. Press "start/stop" to begin.

Nutrition:

- (Per serving) Calories 167 | Fat 7.3g |Sodium 94mg | Carbs 24.9g | Fiber 4.2g | Sugar 6.8g | Protein 2.2g

Quick And Easy Blueberry Muffins

Servings: 8 Muffins
Cooking Time: 12 Minutes
Ingredients:

- 315 ml flour
- 120 ml sugar
- 2 teaspoons baking powder
- ¼ teaspoon salt
- 80 ml rapeseed oil
- 1 egg
- 120 ml milk
- 160 ml blueberries, fresh or frozen and thawed

Directions:

1. Preheat the air fryer to 165ºC.
2. In a medium bowl, stir together flour, sugar, baking powder, and salt.
3. In a separate bowl, combine oil, egg, and milk and mix well.
4. Add egg mixture to dry ingredients and stir just until moistened.
5. Gently stir in the blueberries.
6. Spoon batter evenly into parchment paper-lined muffin cups.
7. Put the muffin cups in the two air fryer baskets and bake for 12 minutes or until tops spring back when touched lightly.
8. Serve immediately.

Sausage And Egg Breakfast Burrito

Servings: 6
Cooking Time: 30 Minutes
Ingredients:

- 6 eggs
- Salt and pepper, to taste
- Cooking oil
- 120 ml chopped red pepper
- 120 ml chopped green pepper
- 230 g chicken sausage meat (removed from casings)
- 120 ml salsa
- 6 medium (8-inch) flour tortillas
- 120 ml shredded Cheddar cheese

Directions:

1. In a medium bowl, whisk the eggs. Add salt and pepper to taste.
2. Place a skillet on medium-high heat. Spray with cooking oil. Add the eggs. Scramble for 2 to 3 minutes, until the eggs are fluffy. Remove the eggs from the skillet and set aside.
3. If needed, spray the skillet with more oil. Add the chopped red and green bell peppers. Cook for 2 to 3 minutes, until the peppers are soft.
4. Add the sausage meat to the skillet. Break the sausage into smaller pieces using a spatula or spoon. Cook for 3 to 4 minutes, until the sausage is brown.
5. Add the salsa and scrambled eggs. Stir to combine. Remove the skillet from heat.
6. Spoon the mixture evenly onto the tortillas.
7. To form the burritos, fold the sides of each tortilla in toward the middle and then roll up from the bottom. You can secure each burrito with a toothpick. Or you can moisten the outside edge of the tortilla with a small amount of water. I prefer to use a cooking brush, but you can also dab with your fingers.
8. Spray the burritos with cooking oil and place them in the two air fryer drawers. Do not stack. Air fry at 204ºC for 8 minutes.
9. Open the air fryer and flip the burritos. Cook for an additional 2 minutes or until crisp.
10. Sprinkle the Cheddar cheese over the burritos. Cool before serving.

Breakfast Meatballs

Servings: 18 Meatballs
Cooking Time: 15 Minutes
Ingredients:

- 450 g pork sausage meat, removed from casings
- ½ teaspoon salt
- ¼ teaspoon ground black pepper
- 120 ml shredded sharp Cheddar cheese
- 30 g cream cheese, softened
- 1 large egg, whisked

Directions:

1. Combine all ingredients in a large bowl. Form mixture into eighteen 1-inch meatballs.
2. Place meatballs into the two ungreased air fryer drawers. Adjust the temperature to 204ºC and air fry for 15 minutes, shaking drawers three times during cooking. Meatballs will be browned on the outside and have an internal temperature of at least 64ºC when completely cooked. Serve warm.

Homemade Toaster Pastries

Servings: 6 Pastries
Cooking Time: 11 Minutes
Ingredients:

- Oil, for spraying
- 1 (425 g) package refrigerated piecrust
- 6 tablespoons jam or preserves of choice
- 475 ml icing sugar
- 3 tablespoons milk
- 1 to 2 tablespoons sprinkles of choice

Directions:

1. Preheat the air fryer to 176ºC. Line the zone 1 air fryer drawer with parchment and spray lightly with oil.
2. Cut the piecrust into 12 rectangles, about 3 by 4 inches each. You will need to reroll the dough scraps to get 12 rectangles.
3. Spread 1 tablespoon of jam in the center of 6 rectangles, leaving ¼ inch around the edges.
4. Pour some water into a small bowl. Use your finger to moisten the edge of each rectangle.
5. Top each rectangle with another and use your fingers to press around the edges. Using the tines of a fork, seal the edges of the dough and poke a few holes in the top of each one. Place the pastries in the prepared drawer.
6. Air fry for 11 minutes. Let cool completely.
7. In a medium bowl, whisk together the icing sugar and milk. Spread the icing over the tops of the pastries and add sprinkles. Serve immediately.

Lemon-blueberry Muffins

Servings: 6 Muffins
Cooking Time: 20 To 25 Minutes
Ingredients:

- 300 ml almond flour
- 3 tablespoons granulated sweetener
- 1 teaspoon baking powder
- 2 large eggs
- 3 tablespoons melted butter
- 1 tablespoon almond milk
- 1 tablespoon fresh lemon juice
- 120 ml fresh blueberries

Directions:

1. Preheat the zone 1 air fryer drawer to 176ºC. Lightly coat 6 silicone muffin cups with vegetable oil. Set aside.
2. In a large mixing bowl, combine the almond flour, sweetener, and baking soda. Set aside.
3. In a separate small bowl, whisk together the eggs, butter, milk, and lemon juice. Add the egg mixture to the flour mixture and stir until just combined. Fold in the blueberries and let the batter sit for 5 minutes.
4. Spoon the muffin batter into the muffin cups, about two-thirds full. Air fry in the zone 1 drawer for 20 to 25 minutes, or until a toothpick inserted into the center of a muffin comes out clean.
5. Remove the drawer from the air fryer and let the muffins cool for about 5 minutes before transferring them to a wire rack to cool completely.

Spinach Omelet And Bacon, Egg, And Cheese Roll Ups

Servings: 6

Cooking Time: 15 Minutes

Ingredients:

- Spinach Omelet:
- 4 large eggs
- 350 ml chopped fresh spinach leaves
- 2 tablespoons peeled and chopped brown onion
- 2 tablespoons salted butter, melted
- 120 ml shredded mild Cheddar cheese
- ¼ teaspoon salt
- Bacon, Egg, and Cheese Roll Ups:
- 2 tablespoons unsalted butter
- 60 ml chopped onion
- ½ medium green pepper, seeded and chopped
- 6 large eggs
- 12 slices bacon
- 235 ml shredded sharp Cheddar cheese
- 120 ml mild salsa, for dipping

Directions:

1. Make the Spinach Omelet :

2. In an ungreased round nonstick baking dish, whisk eggs. Stir in spinach, onion, butter, Cheddar, and salt.

3. Place dish into zone 1 air fryer basket. Adjust the temperature to 160ºC and bake for 12 minutes. Omelet will be done when browned on the top and firm in the middle.

4. Slice in half and serve warm on two medium plates.

5. Make the Bacon, Egg, and Cheese Roll Ups :

6. In a medium skillet over medium heat, melt butter. Add onion and pepper to the skillet and sauté until fragrant and onions are translucent, about 3 minutes.

7. Whisk eggs in a small bowl and pour into skillet. Scramble eggs with onions and peppers until fluffy and fully cooked, about 5 minutes. Remove from heat and set aside.

8. On work surface, place three slices of bacon side by side, overlapping about ¼ inch. Place 60 ml scrambled eggs in a heap on the side closest to you and sprinkle 60 ml cheese on top of the eggs.

9. Tightly roll the bacon around the eggs and secure the seam with a toothpick if necessary. Place each roll into the zone 2 air fryer basket.

10. Adjust the temperature to 175ºC and air fry for 15 minutes. Rotate the rolls halfway through the cooking time.

11. Bacon will be brown and crispy when completely cooked. Serve immediately with salsa for dipping.

Bacon & Spinach Cups

Servings: 6
Cooking Time: 19 Minutes
Ingredients:

- 6 eggs
- 12 bacon slices, chopped
- 120g fresh baby spinach

- 180g heavy cream
- 6 tablespoons Parmesan cheese, grated
- Salt and ground black pepper, as required

Directions:

1. Heat a non-stick frying pan over medium-high heat and cook the bacon for about 6-8 minutes.
2. Add the spinach and cook for about 2-3 minutes.
3. Stir in the heavy cream and Parmesan cheese and cook for about 2-3 minutes.
4. Remove from the heat and set aside to cool slightly.
5. Press "Zone 1" and "Zone 2" of Ninja Foodi 2-Basket Air Fryer and then rotate the knob for each zone to select "Air Fry".
6. Set the temperature to 175 degrees C and then set the time for 5 minutes to preheat.
7. Crack 1 egg in each of 6 greased ramekins and top with bacon mixture.
8. After preheating, arrange 3 ramekins into the basket of each zone.
9. Slide the basket into the Air Fryer and set the time for 5 minutes.
10. After cooking time is completed, remove the ramekins from Air Fryer.
11. Sprinkle the top of each cup with salt and black pepper and serve hot.

Red Pepper And Feta Frittata And Bacon Eggs On The Go

Servings: 5
Cooking Time: 20 Minutes
Ingredients:

- Red Pepper and Feta Frittata:
- Olive oil cooking spray
- 8 large eggs
- 1 medium red pepper, diced
- ½ teaspoon salt
- ½ teaspoon black pepper

- 1 garlic clove, minced
- 120 ml feta, divided
- Bacon Eggs on the Go:
- 2 eggs
- 110 g bacon, cooked
- Salt and ground black pepper, to taste

Directions:

1. Make the Red Pepper and Feta Frittata :
2. Preheat the air fryer to 180ºC. Lightly coat the inside of a 6-inch round cake pan with olive oil cooking spray.
3. In a large bowl, beat the eggs for 1 to 2 minutes, or until well combined.
4. Add the red pepper, salt, black pepper, and garlic to the eggs, and mix together until the red pepper is distributed throughout.
5. Fold in 60 ml the feta cheese.
6. Pour the egg mixture into the prepared cake pan, and sprinkle the remaining 60 ml feta over the top.
7. Place into the zone 1 air fryer basket and bake for 18 to 20 minutes, or until the eggs are set in the center.
8. Remove from the air fryer and allow to cool for 5 minutes before serving.
9. Make the Bacon Eggs on the Go :
10. Preheat the air fryer to 205ºC. Put liners in a regular cupcake tin.
11. Crack an egg into each of the cups and add the bacon. Season with some pepper and salt.
12. Bake in the preheated zone 2 air fryer basket for 15 minutes, or until the eggs are set. Serve warm.

Breakfast Sausage Omelet

Servings:2
Cooking Time:8
Ingredients:

- ¼ pound breakfast sausage, cooked and crumbled
- 4 eggs, beaten
- ½ cup pepper Jack cheese blend
- 2 tablespoons green bell pepper, sliced
- 1 green onion, chopped
- 1 pinch cayenne pepper
- Cooking spray

Directions:

1. Take a bowl and whisk eggs in it along with crumbled sausage, pepper Jack cheese, green onions, red bell pepper, and cayenne pepper.
2. Mix it all well.
3. Take two cake pans that fit inside the air fryer and grease it with oil spray.
4. Divide the omelet mixture between cake pans.
5. Put the cake pans inside both of the Ninja Foodie 2-Basket Air Fryer baskets.
6. Turn on the BAKE function of the zone 1 basket and let it cook for 15-20 minutes at 310 degrees F.
7. Select MATCH button for zone 2 basket.
8. Once the cooking cycle completes, take out, and serve hot, as a delicious breakfast.

Nutrition:

- (Per serving) Calories 691| Fat52.4g | Sodium1122 mg | Carbs 13.3g | Fiber 1.8g| Sugar 7g | Protein 42g

Cinnamon Toast

Servings: 6
Cooking Time: 5 Minutes
Ingredients:

- 12 slices bread
- 115g butter, at room temperature
- 100g white sugar
- 1½ teaspoons ground cinnamon
- 1½ teaspoons pure vanilla extract
- 1 pinch of salt

Directions:

1. Softened butter is mashed with a fork or the back of a spoon, and then sugar, cinnamon, vanilla, and salt are added.
2. Stir everything together thoroughly.
3. Spread one-sixth of the mixture onto each slice of bread, covering the entire surface.
4. Press your chosen zone - "Zone 1" or "Zone 2" and then rotate the knob to select "Air Fryer".
5. Set the temperature to 200 degrees C, and then set the time for 3 minutes to preheat.
6. After preheating, arrange bread into the basket of each zone.
7. Slide the basket into the Air Fryer and set the time for 5 minutes.
8. After cooking time is completed, remove both baskets from Air Fryer.
9. Cut bread slices diagonally and serve.

Spinach And Red Pepper Egg Cups With Coffee-glazed Canadian Bacon

Servings:6

Cooking Time: 13 Minutes

Ingredients:

- FOR THE EGG CUPS
- 4 large eggs
- ¼ cup heavy (whipping) cream
- ¼ teaspoon kosher salt
- ¼ teaspoon freshly ground black pepper
- ½ cup roasted red peppers (about 1 whole pepper), drained and chopped
- ½ cup baby spinach, chopped
- FOR THE CANADIAN BACON
- ¼ cup brewed coffee
- 2 tablespoons maple syrup
- 1 tablespoon light brown sugar
- 6 slices Canadian bacon

Directions:

1. To prep the egg cups: In a medium bowl, whisk together the eggs and cream until well combined with a uniform, light color. Stir in the salt, black pepper, roasted red peppers, and spinach until combined.
2. Divide the egg mixture among 6 silicone muffin cups.
3. To prep the Canadian bacon: In a small bowl, whisk together the coffee, maple syrup, and brown sugar.
4. Using a basting brush, brush the glaze onto both sides of each slice of bacon.
5. To cook the egg cups and Canadian bacon: Install a crisper plate in each of the two baskets. Place the egg cups in the Zone 1 basket and insert the basket in the unit. Place the glazed bacon in the Zone 2 basket, making sure the slices don't overlap, and insert the basket in the unit. It is okay if the bacon overlaps a little bit.
6. Select Zone 1, select BAKE, set the temperature to 325°F, and set the time to 13 minutes.
7. Select Zone 2, select AIR FRY, set the temperature to 400°F, and set the time to 5 minutes. Select SMART FINISH.
8. Press START/PAUSE to begin cooking.
9. When the Zone 2 timer reads 2 minutes, press START/PAUSE. Remove the basket and use silicone-tipped tongs to flip the bacon. Reinsert the basket and press START/PAUSE to resume cooking.
10. When cooking is complete, serve the egg cups with the Canadian bacon.

Nutrition:

- (Per serving) Calories: 180; Total fat: 9.5g; Saturated fat: 4.5g; Carbohydrates: 9g; Fiber: 0g; Protein: 14g; Sodium: 688mg

Hard Boiled Eggs

Servings: 6
Cooking Time: 18 Minutes
Ingredients:

- 6 eggs
- Cold water

Directions:

1. Press your chosen zone - "Zone 1" or "Zone 2" and then rotate the knob to select "Air Fryer".
2. Set the temperature to 120 degrees C, and then set the time for 5 minutes to preheat.
3. After preheating, arrange eggs into the basket of each zone.
4. Slide the baskets into Air Fryer and set the time for 18 minutes.
5. After cooking time is completed, transfer the eggs into cold water and serve.

Baked Peach Oatmeal

Servings: 6
Cooking Time: 30 Minutes
Ingredients:

- Olive oil cooking spray
- 475 ml certified gluten-free rolled oats
- 475 ml unsweetened almond milk
- 60 ml honey, plus more for drizzling (optional)
- 120 ml non-fat plain Greek yoghurt
- 1 teaspoon vanilla extract
- ½ teaspoon ground cinnamon
- ¼ teaspoon salt
- 350 ml diced peaches, divided, plus more for serving (optional)

Directions:

1. Lightly coat the inside of a 6-inch cake pan with olive oil cooking spray. In a large bowl, mix together the oats, almond milk, honey, yoghurt, vanilla, cinnamon, and salt until well combined.

2. Fold in 180 ml peaches and then pour the mixture into the prepared cake pan. Sprinkle the remaining peaches across the top of the oatmeal mixture.

3. Place the cake pan into the zone 1 drawer and bake at 190ºC for 30 minutes. Allow to set and cool for 5 minutes before serving with additional fresh fruit and honey for drizzling, if desired.

Sausage With Eggs

Servings:2
Cooking Time:13
Ingredients:

- 4 sausage links, raw and uncooked
- 4 eggs, uncooked
- 1 tablespoon of green onion
- 2 tablespoons of chopped tomatoes
- Salt and black pepper, to taste
- 2 tablespoons of milk, dairy
- Oil spray, for greasing

Directions:

1. Take a bowl and whisk eggs in it.
2. Then pour milk, and add onions and tomatoes.
3. Whisk it all well.
4. Now season it with salt and black pepper.
5. Take one cake pan, that fit inside the air fryer and grease it with oil spray.
6. Pour the omelet in the greased cake pans.
7. Put the cake pan inside zone 1 air fryer basket of Ninja Foodie 2-Basket Air Fryer.
8. Now place the sausage link into the zone 2 basket.
9. Select bake for zone 1 basket and set the timer to 8-10 minutes at 300 degrees F.
10. For the zone 2 basket, select the AIR FRY button and set the timer to 12 minutes at 390 degrees.
11. Once the cooking cycle completes, serve by transferring it to plates.
12. Chop the sausage or cut it in round and then mix it with omelet.
13. Enjoy hot as a delicious breakfast.

Nutrition:

- (Per serving) Calories 240 | Fat 18.4g| Sodium 396mg | Carbs 2.8g | Fiber0.2g | Sugar 2g | Protein 15.6g

Parmesan Sausage Egg Muffins

Servings: 4
Cooking Time: 20 Minutes
Ingredients:

- 170 g Italian-seasoned sausage, sliced
- 6 eggs
- 30 ml double cream
- Salt and ground black pepper, to taste
- 85 g Parmesan cheese, grated

Directions:

1. Preheat the air fryer to 176°C. Grease a muffin pan.
2. Put the sliced sausage in the muffin pan.
3. Beat the eggs with the cream in a bowl and season with salt and pepper.
4. Pour half of the mixture over the sausages in the pan.
5. Sprinkle with cheese and the remaining egg mixture.
6. Bake in the preheated air fryer for 20 minutes or until set.
7. Serve immediately.

Asparagus And Bell Pepper Strata And Greek Bagels

Servings: 6

Cooking Time: 14 To 20 Minutes

Ingredients:

- Asparagus and Bell Pepper Strata:
- 8 large asparagus spears, trimmed and cut into 2-inch pieces
- 80 ml shredded carrot
- 120 ml chopped red pepper
- 2 slices wholemeal bread, cut into ½-inch cubes
- 3 egg whites
- 1 egg
- 3 tablespoons 1% milk
- ½ teaspoon dried thyme
- Greek Bagels:
- 120 ml self-raising flour, plus more for dusting
- 120 ml plain Greek yoghurt
- 1 egg
- 1 tablespoon water
- 4 teaspoons sesame seeds or za'atar
- Cooking oil spray
- 1 tablespoon butter, melted

Directions:

1. Make the Asparagus and Bell Pepper Strata :
2. In a baking pan, combine the asparagus, carrot, red bell pepper, and 1 tablespoon of water. Bake in the air fryer at 166ºC for 3 to 5 minutes, or until crisp-tender. Drain well.
3. Add the bread cubes to the vegetables and gently toss.
4. In a medium bowl, whisk the egg whites, egg, milk, and thyme until frothy.
5. Pour the egg mixture into the pan. Bake in the zone 1 drawer for 11 to 15 minutes, or until the strata is slightly puffy and set and the top starts to brown. Serve.
6. Make the Greek Bagels :
7. In a large bowl, using a wooden spoon, stir together the flour and yoghurt until a tacky dough forms. Transfer the dough to a lightly floured work surface and roll the dough into a ball.
8. Cut the dough into 2 pieces and roll each piece into a log. Form each log into a bagel shape, pinching the ends together.
9. In a small bowl, whisk the egg and water. Brush the egg wash on the bagels.
10. Sprinkle 2 teaspoons of the toppings on each bagel and gently press it into the dough.
11. Insert the crisper plate into the zone 2 drawer and the drawer into the unit. Preheat the drawer by selecting BAKE, setting the temperature to 166ºC, and setting the time to 3 minutes. Select START/STOP to begin.
12. Once the drawer is preheated, spray the crisper plate with cooking spray. Drizzle the bagels with the butter and place them into the drawer.
13. Select BAKE, set the temperature to 166ºC, and set the time to 10 minutes. Select START/STOP to begin.
14. When the cooking is complete, the bagels should be lightly golden on the outside. Serve warm.

Banana Bread

Servings: 8
Cooking Time: 35 Minutes

Ingredients:

- 95g flour
- 1 teaspoon ground cinnamon
- ¼ teaspoon ground nutmeg
- ½ teaspoon salt
- ¼ teaspoon baking soda
- 2 medium-sized ripe bananas mashed
- 2 large eggs lightly beaten
- 100g granulated sugar
- 2 tablespoons whole milk
- 1 tablespoon plain nonfat yoghurt
- 2 tablespoons vegetable oil
- 1 teaspoon vanilla
- 2 tablespoons walnuts roughly chopped

Directions:

1. Combine flour, cinnamon, nutmeg, baking soda, and salt in a large mixing basin.
2. Mash the banana in a separate dish before adding the eggs, sugar, milk, yoghurt, oil, and vanilla extract.
3. Combine the wet and dry ingredients in a mixing bowl and stir until just incorporated.
4. Pour the batter into the loaf pan and top with chopped walnuts.
5. Press either "Zone 1" and "Zone 2" and then rotate the knob select "Air Fryer".
6. Set the temperature to 155 degrees C, and then set the time for 3 minutes to preheat.
7. After preheating, arrange 1 loaf pan into the basket.
8. Slide basket into Air Fryer and set the time for 35 minutes.
9. After cooking time is completed, remove pan from Air Fryer.
10. Place the loaf pan onto a wire rack to cool for about 10 minutes.
11. Carefully invert the bread onto a wire rack to cool completely before slicing
12. Cut the bread into desired-sized slices and serve.

Wholemeal Banana-walnut Bread

Servings: 6
Cooking Time: 23 Minutes
Ingredients:

- Olive oil cooking spray
- 2 ripe medium bananas
- 1 large egg
- 60 ml non-fat plain Greek yoghurt
- 60 ml olive oil
- ½ teaspoon vanilla extract
- 2 tablespoons honey
- 235 ml wholemeal flour
- ¼ teaspoon salt
- ¼ teaspoon baking soda
- ½ teaspoon ground cinnamon
- 60 ml chopped walnuts

Directions:

1. Lightly coat the inside of two 5 ½-by-3-inch loaf pans with olive oil cooking spray.

2. In a large bowl, mash the bananas with a fork. Add the egg, yoghurt, olive oil, vanilla, and honey. Mix until well combined and mostly smooth. Sift the wholemeal flour, salt, baking soda, and cinnamon into the wet mixture, then stir until just combined. Do not overmix. Gently fold in the walnuts. Pour into the prepared loaf pans and spread to distribute evenly.

3. Place a loaf pan in the zone 1 drawer and another pan into zone 2 drawer. In zone 1, select Bake button and adjust temperature to 180°C, set time to 20 to 23 minutes. In zone 2, select Match Cook and press Start.

4. Remove until golden brown on top and a toothpick inserted into the center comes out clean. Allow to cool for 5 minutes before serving.

Honey-apricot Granola With Greek Yoghurt

Servings: 6
Cooking Time: 30 Minutes
Ingredients:

- 235 ml rolled oats
- 60 ml dried apricots, diced
- 60 ml almond slivers
- 60 ml walnuts, chopped
- 60 ml pumpkin seeds
- 60 to 80 ml honey, plus more for drizzling
- 1 tablespoon olive oil
- 1 teaspoon ground cinnamon
- ¼ teaspoon ground nutmeg
- ¼ teaspoon salt
- 2 tablespoons sugar-free dark chocolate chips (optional)
- 700 ml fat-free plain Greek yoghurt

Directions:

1. Line the zone 1 and zone 2 drawer with two parchment papers. In a large bowl, combine the oats, apricots, almonds, walnuts, pumpkin seeds, honey, olive oil, cinnamon, nutmeg, and salt, mixing so that the honey, oil, and spices are well distributed. Pour the mixture onto the parchment papers and spread it into an even layer.

2. Bake at 130°C for 10 minutes, then shake or stir and spread back out into an even layer. Continue baking for 10 minutes more, then repeat the process of shaking or stirring the mixture.

3. Bake for an additional 10 minutes before removing from the air fryer. Allow the granola to cool completely before stirring in the chocolate chips and pouring into an airtight container for storage. For each serving, top 120 ml Greek yoghurt with 80 ml granola and a drizzle of honey, if needed.

Bacon And Spinach Egg Muffins

Servings: 6
Cooking Time: 12 To 14 Minutes
Ingredients:

- 6 large eggs
- 60 ml double (whipping) cream
- ½ teaspoon sea salt
- ¼ teaspoon freshly ground black pepper
- ¼ teaspoon cayenne pepper (optional)
- 180 ml frozen chopped spinach, thawed and drained
- 4 strips cooked bacon, crumbled
- 60 g shredded Cheddar cheese

Directions:

1. In a large bowl , whisk together the eggs, double cream, salt, black pepper, and cayenne pepper .
2. Divide the spinach and bacon among 6 silicone muffin cups. Place the muffin cups in the zone 1 air fryer drawer.
3. Divide the egg mixture among the muffin cups. Top with the cheese.
4. Set the temperature to 150ºC. Bake for 12 to 14 minutes, until the eggs are set and cooked through.

Snacks And Appetizers Recipes
Five-ingredient Falafel With Garlic-yoghurt Sauce

Servings: 4
Cooking Time: 15 Minutes
Ingredients:

- Falafel:
- 1 (425 g) can chickpeas, drained and rinsed
- 120 ml fresh parsley
- 2 garlic cloves, minced
- ½ tablespoon ground cumin
- 1 tablespoon wholemeal flour
- Salt
- Garlic-Yoghurt Sauce:
- 240 ml non-fat plain Greek yoghurt
- 1 garlic clove, minced
- 1 tablespoon chopped fresh dill
- 2 tablespoons lemon juice

Directions:

1. Make the Falafel: Preheat the air fryer to 180ºC. 2. Put the chickpeas into a food processor. Pulse until mostly chopped, then add the parsley, garlic, and cumin and pulse for another 1 to 2 minutes, or until the ingredients are combined and turning into a dough. 3. Add the flour. Pulse a few more times until combined. The dough will have texture, but the chickpeas should be pulsed into small bits. 4. Using clean hands, roll the dough into 8 balls of equal size, then pat the balls down a bit so they are about ½-thick disks. 5. Spray the zone 1 air fryer basket with olive oil cooking spray, then place the falafel patties in the basket in a single layer, making sure they don't touch each other. 6. Fry in the air fryer for 15 minutes. Make the garlic-yoghurt sauce 7. In a small bowl, combine the yoghurt, garlic, dill, and lemon juice. 8. Once the falafel is done cooking and nicely browned on all sides, remove them from the air fryer and season with salt. 9. Serve hot with a side of dipping sauce.

Onion Pakoras

Servings: 2
Cooking Time: 10 Minutes
Ingredients:

- 2 medium brown or white onions, sliced (475 ml)
- 120 ml chopped fresh coriander
- 2 tablespoons vegetable oil
- 1 tablespoon chickpea flour
- 1 tablespoon rice flour, or 2 tablespoons chickpea flour
- 1 teaspoon ground turmeric
- 1 teaspoon cumin seeds
- 1 teaspoon rock salt
- ½ teaspoon cayenne pepper
- Vegetable oil spray

Directions:

1. In a large bowl, combine the onions, coriander, oil, chickpea flour, rice flour, turmeric, cumin seeds, salt, and cayenne. Stir to combine. Cover and let stand for 30 minutes or up to overnight. Mix well before using.
2. Spray the air fryer baskets generously with vegetable oil spray. Drop the batter in 6 heaping tablespoons into the two baskets. Set the air fryer to 175ºC for 8 minutes. Carefully turn the pakoras over and spray with oil spray. Set the air fryer for 2 minutes, or until the batter is cooked through and crisp, checking at 6 minutes for doneness. Serve hot.

Cinnamon-apple Crisps

Servings: 4
Cooking Time: 32 Minutes
Ingredients:

- Oil, for spraying
- 2 Red Delicious or Honeycrisp apples
- ¼ teaspoon ground cinnamon, divided

Directions:

1. Line the two air fryer baskets with parchment and spray lightly with oil.
2. Trim the uneven ends off the apples. Using a mandoline slicer on the thinnest setting or a sharp knife, cut the apples into very thin slices. Discard the cores.
3. Place the apple slices in a single layer in the two prepared baskets and sprinkle with the cinnamon.
4. Place two metal air fryer trivets on top of the apples to keep them from flying around while they are cooking.
5. Air fry at 150ºC for 16 minutes, flipping every 5 minutes to ensure even cooking.
6. Let cool to room temperature before serving. The crisps will firm up as they cool.

Shrimp Pirogues

Servings: 8
Cooking Time: 4 To 5 Minutes
Ingredients:

- 340 g small, peeled, and deveined raw shrimp
- 85 g soft white cheese, room temperature
- 2 tablespoons natural yoghurt
- 1 teaspoon lemon juice
- 1 teaspoon dried dill weed, crushed
- Salt, to taste
- 4 small hothouse cucumbers, each approximately 6 inches long

Directions:

1. Pour 4 tablespoons water in bottom of air fryer drawer.
2. Place shrimp in air fryer basket in single layer and air fry at 200ºC for 4 to 5 minutes, just until done. Watch carefully because shrimp cooks quickly, and overcooking makes it tough.
3. Chop shrimp into small pieces, no larger than ½ inch. Refrigerate while mixing the remaining ingredients.
4. With a fork, mash and whip the soft white cheese until smooth.
5. Stir in the yoghurt and beat until smooth. Stir in lemon juice, dill weed, and chopped shrimp.
6. Taste for seasoning. If needed, add ¼ to ½ teaspoon salt to suit your taste.
7. Store in refrigerator until serving time.
8. When ready to serve, wash and dry cucumbers and split them lengthwise. Scoop out the seeds and turn cucumbers upside down on paper towels to drain for 10 minutes.
9. Just before filling, wipe centres of cucumbers dry. Spoon the shrimp mixture into the pirogues and cut in half crosswise. Serve immediately.

Pretzels

Servings: 8
Cooking Time: 6 Minutes
Ingredients:

- 360ml warm water
- 1 tablespoon dry active yeast
- 1 tablespoon sugar
- 1 tablespoon olive oil
- 500g plain flour
- 1 teaspoon salt
- 1 large egg
- 1 tablespoon water

Directions:

1. Combine warm water, yeast, sugar, and olive oil in a large mixing bowl. Stir everything together and leave aside for about 5 minutes.
2. Add 375g flour and a teaspoon of salt to the mixture. Stir well.
3. On a floured surface, roll out the dough. Knead for 3 to 5 minutes, or until the dough is no longer sticky, adding flour 1 tablespoon at a time if necessary.
4. The dough should be divided in half. At a time, work with half of the dough.
5. Each dough half should be divided into eight pieces.
6. Make a 45cm rope out of the dough. Make a U shape out of the dough. Twist the ends two more times.
7. Fold the ends of the dough over the spherical portion.
8. In a small mixing dish, whisk the egg and a tablespoon of water.
9. Brush the egg wash on both sides of the pretzel dough.
10. Press your chosen zone - "Zone 1" or "Zone 2" and then rotate the knob to select "Air Fryer".
11. Set the temperature to 185 degrees C, and then set the time for 5 minutes to preheat.
12. After preheating, arrange pretzels into the basket of each zone.
13. Slide the baskets into Air Fryer and set the time for 6 minutes.
14. After cooking time is completed, place on a wire rack for a few minutes, then transfer onto serving plates and serve.

Cauliflower Gnocchi

Servings: 5
Cooking Time: 17 Minutes.
Ingredients:

- 1 bag frozen cauliflower gnocchi
- 1 ½ tablespoons olive oil
- 1 teaspoon garlic powder
- 3 tablespoons parmesan, grated
- ½ teaspoon dried basil
- Salt to taste
- Fresh chopped parsley for topping

Directions:

1. Toss gnocchi with olive oil, garlic powder, 1 tablespoon of parmesan, salt, and basil in a bowl.
2. Divide the gnocchi in the two crisper plate.
3. Return the crisper plate to the Ninja Foodi Dual Zone Air Fryer.
4. Choose the Air Fry mode for Zone 1 and set the temperature to 400 degrees F and the time to 10 minutes.
5. Select the "MATCH" button to copy the settings for Zone 2.
6. Initiate cooking by pressing the START/STOP button.
7. Toss the gnocchi once cooked halfway through, then resume cooking.
8. Drizzle the remaining parmesan on top of the gnocchi and cook again for 7 minutes.
9. Serve warm.

Nutrition:

- (Per serving) Calories 134 | Fat 5.9g |Sodium 343mg | Carbs 9.5g | Fiber 0.5g | Sugar 1.1g | Protein 10.4g

Croquettes

Servings: 6
Cooking Time: 10 Minutes
Ingredients:

- 460g mashed potatoes
- 50g grated Parmesan cheese
- 50g shredded Swiss cheese
- 1 shallot, finely chopped
- 2 teaspoons minced fresh rosemary
- ½ teaspoon salt
- ¼ teaspoon pepper
- 420g finely chopped cooked turkey
- 1 large egg
- 2 tablespoons water
- 110g panko bread crumbs
- Cooking spray

Directions:

1. Combine mashed potatoes, cheeses, shallot, rosemary, salt, and pepper in a large mixing bowl| stir in turkey.
2. Lightly but completely combine the ingredients. Form into twelve 5cm thick patties.
3. Whisk the egg and water together in a small basin. In a shallow bowl, place the bread crumbs.
4. Dip the croquettes in the egg mixture, then in the bread crumbs, patting them down.
5. Press either "Zone 1" or "Zone 2" and then rotate the knob to select "Air Fry".
6. Set the temperature to 190 degrees C, and then set the time for 5 minutes to preheat.
7. After preheating, spray the Air-Fryer basket with cooking spray and line with parchment paper. Arrange in a single layer and spritz them with cooking spray.
8. Slide the basket into the Air Fryer and set the time for 5 minutes.
9. After that, turn them and again cook for 5 minutes longer.
10. After cooking time is completed, transfer them onto serving plates and serve.

Bruschetta With Basil Pesto

Servings: 4
Cooking Time: 5 To 11 Minutes
Ingredients:
- 8 slices French bread, ½ inch thick
- 2 tablespoons softened butter
- 240 ml shredded Mozzarella cheese
- 120 ml basil pesto
- 240 ml chopped grape tomatoes
- 2 spring onions, thinly sliced

Directions:
1. Preheat the air fryer to 175ºC.
2. Spread the bread with the butter and place butter-side up in the two air fryer baskets. Bake for 3 to 5 minutes, or until the bread is light golden brown.
3. Remove the bread from the baskets and top each piece with some of the cheese. Return to the baskets in 2 baskets and bake for 1 to 3 minutes, or until the cheese melts.
4. Meanwhile, combine the pesto, tomatoes, and spring onions in a small bowl.
5. When the cheese has melted, remove the bread from the air fryer and place on a serving plate. Top each slice with some of the pesto mixture and serve.

Pumpkin Fries

Servings: 4
Cooking Time: 15 Minutes
Ingredients:
- 120g plain Greek yoghurt
- 2 to 3 teaspoons minced chipotle peppers
- ⅛ teaspoon plus ½ teaspoon salt, divided
- 1 medium pie pumpkin
- ¼ teaspoon garlic powder
- ¼ teaspoon ground cumin
- ¼ teaspoon chili powder
- ¼ teaspoon pepper

Directions:
1. Combine yoghurt, chipotle peppers, and ⅛ teaspoon salt in a small bowl. Refrigerate until ready to serve, covered.
2. Peeled the pumpkin and split it in half lengthwise. Discard the seeds. Cut pumpkin into 1 cm strips.
3. Place in a large mixing bowl. Toss with ½ teaspoon salt, garlic powder, cumin, chili powder, and pepper.
4. Press either "Zone 1" or "Zone 2" and then rotate the knob to select "Air Fry".
5. Set the temperature to 200 degrees C, and then set the time for 5 minutes to preheat.
6. After preheating, spray the Air-Fryer basket with cooking spray and line with parchment paper. Arrange pumpkin fries and spritz cooking spray on them.
7. Slide the basket into the Air Fryer and set the time for 8 minutes.
8. After that, toss them and again cook for 3 minutes longer.
9. After cooking time is completed, transfer them onto serving plates and serve.

Mushroom Rolls

Servings: 10
Cooking Time: 10 Minutes
Ingredients:

- 2 tablespoons olive oil
- 200g large portobello mushrooms, finely chopped
- 1 teaspoon dried oregano
- ½ teaspoon crushed red pepper flakes
- ¼ teaspoon salt
- 200g cream cheese, softened
- 100g whole-milk ricotta cheese
- 10 flour tortillas
- Cooking spray

Directions:

1. Heat the oil in a frying pan over medium heat. Add the mushrooms and cook for 4 minutes.
2. Sauté until mushrooms are browned, about 4-6 minutes, with oregano, pepper flakes, and salt. Cool.
3. Combine the cheeses in a mixing bowl| fold the mushrooms until thoroughly combined. On the bottom centre of each tortilla, spread 3 tablespoons of the mushroom mixture. Tightly roll up and secure with toothpicks.
4. Press either "Zone 1" or "Zone 2" and then rotate the knob to select "Air Fry".
5. Set the temperature to 200 degrees C, and then set the time for 5 minutes to preheat.
6. After preheating, spray the basket with cooking spray and arrange rolls onto basket.
7. Slide the basket into the Air Fryer and set the time for 10 minutes.
8. After cooking time is completed, transfer them onto serving plates and serve.

Crispy Calamari Rings

Servings: 4
Cooking Time: 10 Minutes
Ingredients:

- 455g calamari rings, patted dry
- 3 tablespoons lemon juice
- 60g plain flour
- 1 teaspoon garlic powder
- 2 egg whites
- 60ml milk
- 220g panko breadcrumbs
- 1½ teaspoon salt
- 1½ teaspoon ground black pepper

Directions:

1. Allow the squid rings to marinade for at least 30 minutes in a bowl with lemon juice. Drain the water in a colander.
2. In a shallow bowl, combine the flour and garlic powder.
3. In a separate bowl, whisk together the egg whites and milk.
4. In a third bowl, combine the panko breadcrumbs, salt, and pepper.
5. Floured first the calamari rings, then dip in the egg mixture, and finally in the panko breadcrumb mixture.
6. Press either "Zone 1" or "Zone 2" and then rotate the knob to select "Air Fry".
7. Set the temperature to 200 degrees C, and then set the time for 5 minutes to preheat.
8. After preheating, spray the Air-Fryer basket with cooking spray and line with parchment paper. Arrange in a single layer and spritz them with cooking spray.
9. Slide the basket into the Air Fryer and set the time for 10 minutes.
10. After cooking time is completed, transfer them onto serving plates and serve.

Cheese Drops

Servings: 8
Cooking Time: 10 Minutes
Ingredients:

- 177 ml plain flour
- ½ teaspoon rock salt
- ¼ teaspoon cayenne pepper
- ¼ teaspoon smoked paprika
- ¼ teaspoon black pepper
- Dash garlic powder (optional)
- 60 ml butter, softened
- 240 ml shredded extra mature Cheddar cheese, at room temperature
- Olive oil spray

Directions:

1. In a small bowl, combine the flour, salt, cayenne, paprika, pepper, and garlic powder, if using. 2. Using a food processor, cream the butter and cheese until smooth. Gently add the seasoned flour and process until the dough is well combined, smooth, and no longer sticky. 3. Divide the dough into 32 equal-size pieces. On a lightly floured surface, roll each piece into a small ball. 4. Spray the two air fryer baskets with oil spray. Arrange the cheese drops in the two baskets. Set the air fryer to 165°C for 10 minutes, or until drops are just starting to brown. Transfer to a wire rack. 5. Cool the cheese drops completely on the wire rack. Store in an airtight container until ready to serve, or up to 1 or 2 days.

Crispy Filo Artichoke Triangles

Servings: 18 Triangles
Cooking Time: 9 To 12 Minutes
Ingredients:

- 60 ml Ricotta cheese
- 1 egg white
- 80 ml minced and drained artichoke hearts
- 3 tablespoons grated Mozzarella cheese
- ½ teaspoon dried thyme
- 6 sheets frozen filo pastry, thawed
- 2 tablespoons melted butter

Directions:

1. Preheat the air fryer to 205°C.
2. In a small bowl, combine the Ricotta cheese, egg white, artichoke hearts, Mozzarella cheese, and thyme, and mix well.
3. Cover the filo pastry with a damp kitchen towel while you work so it doesn't dry out. Using one sheet at a time, place on the work surface and cut into thirds lengthwise.
4. Put about 1½ teaspoons of the filling on each strip at the base. Fold the bottom right-hand tip of phyllo over the filling to meet the other side in a triangle, then continue folding in a triangle. Brush each triangle with butter to seal the edges. Repeat with the remaining phyllo dough and filling.
5. Place the triangles in the two air fryer baskets. Bake, 6 at a time, in two baskets for about 3 to 4 minutes, or until the filo is golden brown and crisp.
6. Serve hot.

Jalapeño Popper Chicken

Servings: 4

Cooking Time: 50 Minutes

Ingredients:

- 2 ounces cream cheese, softened
- ¼ cup shredded cheddar cheese
- ¼ cup shredded mozzarella cheese
- ¼ teaspoon garlic powder
- 4 small jalapeño peppers, seeds removed and diced
- Kosher salt, as desired
- Ground black pepper, as desired
- 4 organic boneless, skinless chicken breasts
- 8 slices bacon

Directions:

1. Cream together the cream cheese, cheddar cheese, mozzarella cheese, garlic powder, and jalapeño in a mixing bowl. Add salt and pepper to taste.

2. Make a deep pocket in the center of each chicken breast, but be cautious not to cut all the way through.

3. Fill each chicken breast's pocket with the cream cheese mixture.

4. Wrap two strips of bacon around each chicken breast and attach them with toothpicks.

5. Place a crisper plate in each drawer. Put the chicken breasts in the drawers. Place both drawers in the unit.

6. Select zone 1, then AIR FRY, and set the temperature to 350 degrees F/ 175 degrees C with a 30-minute timer. To match zone 2 and zone 1 settings, select MATCH. To begin cooking, press the START/STOP button.

7. When cooking is complete, remove the chicken breasts and allow them to rest for 5 minutes before serving

Nutrition:

- (Per serving) Calories 507 | Fat 27.5g | Sodium 1432mg | Carbs 2.3g | Fiber 0.6g | Sugar 0.6g | Protein 58.2g

Blueberries Muffins

Servings:2

Cooking Time:15

Ingredients:

- Salt, pinch
- 2 eggs
- 1/3 cup sugar
- 1/3 cup vegetable oil
- 4 tablespoons of water
- 1 teaspoon of lemon zest
- ¼ teaspoon of vanilla extract
- ½ teaspoon of baking powder
- 1 cup all-purpose flour
- 1 cup blueberries

Directions:

1. Take 4 one-cup sized ramekins that are oven safe and layer them with muffin papers.

2. Take a bowl and whisk the egg, sugar, oil, water, vanilla extract, and lemon zest.

3. Whisk it all very well.

4. Now, in a separate bowl, mix the flour, baking powder, and salt.

5. Now, add dry ingredients slowly to wet ingredients.

6. Now, pour this batter into ramekins and top it with blueberries.

7. Now, divide it between both zones of the Ninja Foodie 2-Basket Air Fryer.

8. Set the time for zone 1 to 15 minutes at 350 degrees F.

9. Select the MATCH button for the zone 2 basket.

10. Check if not done, and let it AIR FRY for one more minute.

11. Once it is done, serve.

Nutrition:

- (Per serving) Calories 781| Fat41.6g | Sodium 143mg | Carbs 92.7g | Fiber 3.5g| Sugar41.2 g | Protein 0g

Taco-spiced Chickpeas And Black Bean Corn Dip

Servings: 7
Cooking Time: 17 Minutes
Ingredients:
- Taco-Spiced Chickpeas:
- Oil, for spraying
- 1 (439 g) can chickpeas, drained
- 1 teaspoon chilli powder
- ½ teaspoon ground cumin
- ½ teaspoon salt
- ½ teaspoon granulated garlic
- 2 teaspoons lime juice
- Black Bean Corn Dip:
- ½ (425 g) can black beans, drained and rinsed
- ½ (425 g) can corn, drained and rinsed
- 60 ml chunky salsa
- 57 g low-fat soft white cheese
- 60 ml shredded low-fat Cheddar cheese
- ½ teaspoon ground cumin
- ½ teaspoon paprika
- Salt and freshly ground black pepper, to taste

Directions:
1. Make the Taco-Spiced Chickpeas :
2. Line the zone 1 air fryer basket with parchment and spray lightly with oil. Place the chickpeas in the prepared basket.
3. Air fry at 200ºC for 17 minutes, shaking or stirring the chickpeas and spraying lightly with oil every 5 to 7 minutes.
4. In a small bowl, mix together the chilli powder, cumin, salt, and garlic.
5. When 2 to 3 minutes of cooking time remain, sprinkle half of the seasoning mix over the chickpeas. Finish cooking.
6. Transfer the chickpeas to a medium bowl and toss with the remaining seasoning mix and the lime juice. Serve immediately.
7. Make the Black Bean Corn Dip :
8. Preheat the air fryer to 165ºC.
9. In a medium bowl, mix together the black beans, corn, salsa, soft white cheese, Cheddar cheese, cumin, and paprika. Season with salt and pepper and stir until well combined.
10. Spoon the mixture into a baking dish.
11. Place baking dish in the zone 2 air fryer basket and bake until heated through, about 10 minutes.
12. Serve hot.

Onion Rings

Servings: 4
Cooking Time: 10 Minutes
Ingredients:

- 170g onion, sliced into rings
- ½ cup breadcrumbs
- 2 eggs, beaten
- ½ cup flour
- Salt and black pepper to taste

Directions:

1. Mix flour, black pepper and salt in a bowl.
2. Dredge the onion rings through the flour mixture.
3. Dip them in the eggs and coat with the breadcrumbs.
4. Place the coated onion rings in the air fryer baskets.
5. Return the air fryer basket 1 to Zone 1, and basket 2 to Zone 2 of the Ninja Foodi 2-Basket Air Fryer.
6. Choose the "Air Fry" mode for Zone 1 at 350 degrees F and 7 minutes of cooking time.
7. Select the "MATCH COOK" option to copy the settings for Zone 2.
8. Initiate cooking by pressing the START/PAUSE BUTTON.
9. Shake the rings once cooked halfway through.
10. Serve warm.

Crunchy Basil White Beans And Artichoke And Olive Pitta Flatbread

Servings: 6
Cooking Time: 19 Minutes
Ingredients:

- Crunchy Basil White Beans:
- 1 (425 g) can cooked white beans
- 2 tablespoons olive oil
- 1 teaspoon fresh sage, chopped
- ¼ teaspoon garlic powder
- ¼ teaspoon salt, divided
- 1 teaspoon chopped fresh basil
- Artichoke and Olive Pitta Flatbread:
- 2 wholewheat pittas
- 2 tablespoons olive oil, divided
- 2 garlic cloves, minced
- ¼ teaspoon salt
- 120 ml canned artichoke hearts, sliced
- 60 ml Kalamata olives
- 60 ml shredded Parmesan
- 60 ml crumbled feta
- Chopped fresh parsley, for garnish (optional)

Directions:

1. Make the Crunchy Basil White Beans :
2. Preheat the air fryer to 190°C.
3. In a medium bowl, mix together the beans, olive oil, sage, garlic, ⅛ teaspoon salt, and basil.
4. Pour the white beans into the air fryer and spread them out in a single layer.
5. Bake in zone 1 basket for 10 minutes. Stir and continue cooking for an additional 5 to 9 minutes, or until they reach your preferred level of crispiness.
6. Toss with the remaining ⅛ teaspoon salt before serving.
7. Make the Artichoke and Olive Pitta Flatbread :
8. Preheat the air fryer to 190°C.
9. Brush each pitta with 1 tablespoon olive oil, then sprinkle the minced garlic and salt over the top.
10. Distribute the artichoke hearts, olives, and cheeses evenly between the two pittas, and place both into the zone 2 air fryer basket to bake for 10 minutes.
11. Remove the pittas and cut them into 4 pieces each before serving. Sprinkle parsley over the top, if desired.

Cauliflower Cheese Patties

Servings: 4

Cooking Time: 10 Minutes

Ingredients:

- 2 eggs
- 200g cauliflower rice, microwave for 5 minutes
- 56g mozzarella cheese, shredded
- 22g parmesan cheese, grated
- 11g Mexican cheese, shredded
- ½ tsp onion powder
- 1 tsp dried basil
- 1 tsp garlic powder
- 33g breadcrumbs
- Pepper
- Salt

Directions:

1. Add cauliflower rice and remaining ingredients into the mixing bowl and mix until well combined.
2. Insert a crisper plate in the Ninja Foodi air fryer baskets.
3. Make patties from the cauliflower mixture and place them in both baskets.
4. Select zone 1, then select "air fry" mode and set the temperature to 390 degrees F for 10 minutes. Press "match" to match zone 2 settings to zone 1. Press "start/stop" to begin. Turn halfway through.

Tasty Sweet Potato Wedges

Servings: 4

Cooking Time: 20 Minutes

Ingredients:

- 2 sweet potatoes, peel & cut into wedges
- 1 tbsp BBQ spice rub
- ½ tsp sweet paprika
- 1 tbsp olive oil
- Pepper
- Salt

Directions:

1. In a bowl, toss sweet potato wedges with sweet paprika, oil, BBQ spice rub, pepper, and salt.
2. Insert a crisper plate in the Ninja Foodi air fryer baskets.
3. Add sweet potato wedges in both baskets.
4. Select zone 1 then select "air fry" mode and set the temperature to 390 degrees F for 20 minutes. Press "match" to match zone 2 settings to zone 1. Press "start/stop" to begin. Turn halfway through.

Potato Tacos

Servings: 6
Cooking Time: 15 Minutes

Ingredients:

- 5 small russet potatoes
- 24 mini corn tortillas
- 2 tablespoons rapeseed oil
- ½ teaspoon ground cumin
- ½ teaspoon smoked paprika
- ½ teaspoon granulated garlic
- Salt and pepper, to taste
- 24 long toothpicks

Directions:

1. Fill a pot halfway with cold water and add entire potatoes. Bring to a boil over high heat, then reduce to medium-high and simmer until fork-tender, about 15 minutes.
2. It takes about 15-20 minutes. Drain and allow to cool slightly before peeling.
3. In a bowl, combine peeled potatoes and seasonings. Mash until the mixture is relatively smooth. Season to taste.
4. Heat tortillas in a large frying pan until warm and malleable. Cover with a towel while you finish heating the rest of the tortillas.
5. On half of a tortilla, spread roughly one heaping tablespoon of mash. Fold it in half and weave a toothpick through it to seal it.
6. Brush the tacos lightly with oil on both sides.
7. Press your chosen zone - "Zone 1" or "Zone 2" and then rotate the knob to select "Air Fryer".
8. Set the temperature to 200 degrees C, and then set the time for 5 minutes to preheat.
9. After preheating, arrange them into the basket of each zone.
10. Slide the baskets into Air Fryer and set the time for 15 minutes.
11. After cooking time is completed, place on a wire rack for a few minutes, then transfer onto serving plates and serve.

Poultry Recipes
Turkey Meatloaf With Veggie Medley

Servings: 4
Cooking Time: 30 Minutes
Ingredients:

- FOR THE MEATLOAF
- 1 large egg
- ¼ cup ketchup
- 2 teaspoons Worcestershire sauce
- ½ cup Italian-style bread crumbs
- 1 teaspoon kosher salt
- 1 pound ground turkey (93 percent lean)
- 1 tablespoon vegetable oil
- FOR THE VEGGIE MEDLEY
- 2 carrots, thinly sliced
- 8 ounces green beans, trimmed (about 2 cups)
- 2 cups broccoli florets
- 1 red bell pepper, sliced into strips
- 2 tablespoons vegetable oil
- ½ teaspoon kosher salt
- ½ teaspoon freshly ground black pepper

Directions:

1. To prep the meatloaf:
2. In a large bowl, whisk the egg. Stir in the ketchup, Worcestershire sauce, bread crumbs, and salt. Let sit for 5 minutes to allow the bread crumbs to absorb some moisture.
3. Gently mix in the turkey until just incorporated. Form the mixture into a loaf. Brush with the oil.
4. To prep the veggie medley: In a large bowl, combine the carrots, green beans, broccoli, bell pepper, oil, salt, and black pepper. Mix well to coat the vegetables with the oil.
5. To cook the meatloaf and veggie medley:
6. Install a crisper plate in each of the two baskets. Place the meatloaf in the Zone 1 basket and insert the basket in the unit. Place the vegetables in the Zone 2 basket and insert the basket in the unit.
7. Select Zone 1, select ROAST, set the temperature to 350°F, and set the time to 30 minutes.
8. Select Zone 2, select AIR FRY, set the temperature to 390°F, and set the time to 20 minutes. Select SMART FINISH.
9. Press START/PAUSE to begin cooking.
10. When cooking is complete, the meatloaf will be cooked through and the vegetables will be tender and roasted.

Bang-bang Chicken

Servings: 2
Cooking Time: 20 Minutes
Ingredients:

- 1 cup mayonnaise
- ½ cup sweet chili sauce
- 2 tablespoons Sriracha sauce
- ⅓ cup flour
- 1 lb. boneless chicken breast, diced
- 1 ½ cups panko bread crumbs
- 2 green onions, chopped

Directions:

1. Mix mayonnaise with Sriracha and sweet chili sauce in a large bowl.
2. Keep ¾ cup of the mixture aside.
3. Add flour, chicken, breadcrumbs, and remaining mayo mixture to a resealable plastic bag.
4. Zip the bag and shake well to coat.
5. Divide the chicken in the two crisper plates in a single layer.
6. Return the crisper plate to the Ninja Foodi Dual Zone Air Fryer.
7. Choose the Air Fry mode for Zone 1 and set the temperature to 390 degrees F and the time to 20 minutes|
8. Select the "MATCH" button to copy the settings for Zone 2.
9. Initiate cooking by pressing the START/STOP button.
10. Flip the chicken once cooked halfway through.
11. Top the chicken with reserved mayo sauce.
12. Garnish with green onions and serve warm.

Curried Orange Honey Chicken

Servings: 4
Cooking Time: 16 To 19 Minutes
Ingredients:

- 340 g boneless, skinless chicken thighs, cut into 1-inch pieces
- 1 yellow bell pepper, cut into 1½-inch pieces
- 1 small red onion, sliced
- Olive oil for misting
- 60 ml chicken stock
- 2 tablespoons honey
- 60 ml orange juice
- 1 tablespoon cornflour
- 2 to 3 teaspoons curry powder

Directions:

1. Preheat the air fryer to 190ºC.
2. Put the chicken thighs, pepper, and red onion in the zone 1 air fryer drawer and mist with olive oil.
3. Roast for 12 to 14 minutes or until the chicken is cooked to 76ºC, shaking the drawer halfway through cooking time.
4. Remove the chicken and vegetables from the air fryer drawer and set aside.
5. In a metal bowl, combine the stock, honey, orange juice, cornflour, and curry powder, and mix well. Add the chicken and vegetables, stir, and put the bowl in the drawer.
6. Return the drawer to the air fryer and roast for 2 minutes. Remove and stir, then roast for 2 to 3 minutes or until the sauce is thickened and bubbly.
7. Serve warm.

Chicken With Bacon And Tomato & Bacon-wrapped Stuffed Chicken Breasts

Servings: 8

Cooking Time: 30 Minutes

Ingredients:

- Chicken with Bacon and Tomato:
- 4 medium-sized skin-on chicken drumsticks
- 1½ teaspoons herbs de Provence
- Salt and pepper, to taste
- 1 tablespoon rice vinegar
- 2 tablespoons olive oil
- 2 garlic cloves, crushed
- 340 g crushed canned tomatoes
- 1 small-size leek, thinly sliced
- 2 slices smoked bacon, chopped
- Bacon-Wrapped Stuffed Chicken Breasts:
- 80 g chopped frozen spinach, thawed and squeezed dry
- 55 g cream cheese, softened
- 20 g grated Parmesan cheese
- 1 jalapeño, seeded and chopped
- ½ teaspoon kosher salt
- 1 teaspoon black pepper
- 2 large boneless, skinless chicken breasts, butterflied and pounded to ½-inch thickness
- 4 teaspoons salt-free Cajun seasoning
- 6 slices bacon

Directions:

1. Make the Chicken with Bacon and Tomato :

2. Sprinkle the chicken drumsticks with herbs de Provence, salt and pepper; then, drizzle them with rice vinegar and olive oil.

3. Place into a baking pan and cook in the zone 1 basket at 180°C for 8 to 10 minutes. Pause the air fryer; stir in the remaining ingredients and continue to cook for 15 minutes longer; make sure to check them periodically. Bon appétit!

4. Make the Bacon-Wrapped Stuffed Chicken Breasts :

5. In a small bowl, combine the spinach, cream cheese, Parmesan cheese, jalapeño, salt, and pepper. Stir until well combined.

6. Place the butterflied chicken breasts on a flat surface. Spread the cream cheese mixture evenly across each piece of chicken. Starting with the narrow end, roll up each chicken breast, ensuring the filling stays inside. Season chicken with the Cajun seasoning, patting it in to ensure it sticks to the meat.

7. Wrap each breast in 3 slices of bacon. Place in the zone 2 air fryer basket. Set the air fryer to 180°C for 30 minutes. Use a meat thermometer to ensure the chicken has reached an internal temperature of 75°C.

8. Let the chicken stand 5 minutes before slicing each rolled-up breast in half to serve.

Turkey And Cranberry Quesadillas

Servings: 4
Cooking Time: 4 To 8 Minutes
Ingredients:

- 6 low-sodium whole-wheat tortillas
- 75 g shredded low-sodium low-fat Swiss cheese
- 105 g shredded cooked low-sodium turkey breast
- 2 tablespoons cranberry sauce
- 2 tablespoons dried cranberries
- ½ teaspoon dried basil
- Olive oil spray, for spraying the tortillas

Directions:

1. Preheat the air fryer to 200ºC.
2. Put 3 tortillas on a work surface.
3. Evenly divide the Swiss cheese, turkey, cranberry sauce, and dried cranberries among the tortillas. Sprinkle with the basil and top with the remaining tortillas.
4. Spray the outsides of the tortillas with olive oil spray.
5. One at a time, air fry the quesadillas in the air fryer for 4 to 8 minutes, or until crisp and the cheese is melted. Cut into quarters and serve.

Goat Cheese–stuffed Chicken Breast With Broiled Zucchini And Cherry Tomatoes

Servings: 4
Cooking Time: 25 Minutes
Ingredients:

- FOR THE STUFFED CHICKEN BREASTS
- 2 ounces soft goat cheese
- 1 tablespoon minced fresh parsley
- ½ teaspoon minced garlic
- 4 boneless, skinless chicken breasts (6 ounces each)
- 1 tablespoon vegetable oil
- ½ teaspoon Italian seasoning
- ½ teaspoon kosher salt
- ½ teaspoon freshly ground black pepper
- FOR THE ZUCCHINI AND TOMATOES
- 1 pound zucchini, diced
- 1 cup cherry tomatoes, halved
- 1 tablespoon vegetable oil
- ½ teaspoon kosher salt
- ¼ teaspoon freshly ground black pepper

Directions:

1. To prep the stuffed chicken breasts:
2. In a small bowl, combine the goat cheese, parsley, and garlic. Mix well.
3. Cut a deep slit into the fatter side of each chicken breast to create a pocket . Stuff each breast with the goat cheese mixture. Use a toothpick to secure the opening of the chicken, if needed.
4. Brush the outside of the chicken breasts with the oil and season with the Italian seasoning, salt, and black pepper.
5. To prep the zucchini and tomatoes: In a large bowl, combine the zucchini, tomatoes, and oil. Mix to coat. Season with salt and black pepper.
6. To cook the chicken and vegetables:
7. Install a crisper plate in each of the two baskets. Insert a broil rack in the Zone 2 basket over the crisper plate. Place the chicken in the Zone 1 basket and insert the basket in the unit. Place the vegetables on the broiler rack in the Zone 2 basket and insert the basket in the unit.
8. Select Zone 1, select AIR FRY, set the temperature to 390°F, and set the time to 25 minutes.
9. Select Zone 2, select AIR BROIL, set the temperature to 450°F, and set the time to 10 minutes. Select SMART FINISH.
10. Press START/PAUSE to begin cooking.
11. When cooking is complete, the chicken will be golden brown and cooked through and the zucchini will be soft and slightly charred. Serve hot.

Juicy Paprika Chicken Breast

Servings: 4
Cooking Time: 30 Minutes
Ingredients:

- Oil, for spraying
- 4 (170 g) boneless, skinless chicken breasts
- 1 tablespoon olive oil
- 1 tablespoon paprika
- 1 tablespoon packed light brown sugar
- ½ teaspoon cayenne pepper
- ½ teaspoon onion powder
- ½ teaspoon granulated garlic

Directions:

1. Line the two air fryer drawers with parchment and spray lightly with oil.
2. Brush the chicken with the olive oil.
3. In a small bowl, mix together the paprika, brown sugar, cayenne pepper, onion powder, and garlic and sprinkle it over the chicken.
4. Place the chicken in the two prepared drawers.
5. Air fry at 180ºC for 15 minutes, flip, and cook for another 15 minutes, or until the internal temperature reaches 76ºC. Serve immediately.

Tex-mex Chicken Roll-ups

Servings: 8
Cooking Time: 14 To 17 Minutes
Ingredients:

- 900 g boneless, skinless chicken breasts or thighs
- 1 teaspoon chili powder
- ½ teaspoon smoked paprika
- ½ teaspoon ground cumin
- Sea salt and freshly ground black pepper, to taste
- 170 g Monterey Jack cheese, shredded
- 115 g canned diced green chilies
- Avocado oil spray

Directions:

1. Place the chicken in a large zip-top bag or between two pieces of plastic wrap. Using a meat mallet or heavy skillet, pound the chicken until it is about ¼ inch thick.
2. In a small bowl, combine the chili powder, smoked paprika, cumin, and salt and pepper to taste. Sprinkle both sides of the chicken with the seasonings.
3. Sprinkle the chicken with the Monterey Jack cheese, then the diced green chilies.
4. Roll up each piece of chicken from the long side, tucking in the ends as you go. Secure the roll-up with a toothpick.
5. Set the air fryer to 180ºC. . Spray the outside of the chicken with avocado oil. Place the chicken in a single layer in the two baskets, and roast for 7 minutes. Flip and cook for another 7 to 10 minutes, until an instant-read thermometer reads 70ºC.
6. Remove the chicken from the air fryer and allow it to rest for about 5 minutes before serving.

Easy Chicken Thighs

Servings: 8
Cooking Time: 12 Minutes
Ingredients:

- 900g chicken thighs, boneless & skinless
- 2 tsp chilli powder
- 2 tsp olive oil
- 1 tsp garlic powder
- 1 tsp ground cumin
- Pepper
- Salt

Directions:

1. In a bowl, mix chicken with remaining ingredients until well coated.
2. Insert a crisper plate in the Ninja Foodi air fryer baskets.
3. Place chicken thighs in both baskets.
4. Select zone 1 then select "air fry" mode and set the temperature to 390 degrees F for 12 minutes. Press "match" to match zone 2 settings to zone 1. Press "start/stop" to begin. Turn halfway through.

Nutrition:

- (Per serving) Calories 230 | Fat 9.7g | Sodium 124mg | Carbs 0.7g | Fiber 0.3g | Sugar 0.2g | Protein 33g

Air Fried Turkey Breast

Servings: 4
Cooking Time: 46 Minutes
Ingredients:

- 2 lbs. turkey breast, on the bone with skin
- ½ tablespoon olive oil
- 1 teaspoon salt
- ¼ tablespoon dry poultry seasoning

Directions:

1. Rub turkey breast with ½ tablespoons of oil.
2. Season both its sides with turkey seasoning and salt, then rub in the brush half tablespoons of oil over the skin of the turkey.
3. Divide the turkey in half and place each half in each of the crisper plate.
4. Return the crisper plate to the Ninja Foodi Dual Zone Air Fryer.
5. Choose the Air Fry mode for Zone 1 and set the temperature to 390 degrees F and the time to 46 minutes|
6. Select the "MATCH" button to copy the settings for Zone 2.
7. Initiate cooking by pressing the START/STOP button.
8. Flip the turkey once cooked halfway through, and resume cooking.
9. Slice and serve warm.

Delicious Chicken Skewers

Servings: 4
Cooking Time: 15 Minutes
Ingredients:

- 900g chicken thighs, cut into cubes
- 45ml fresh lime juice
- 59ml coconut milk
- 2 tbsp Thai red curry
- 35ml maple syrup
- 120ml tamari soy sauce

Directions:

1. Add chicken and remaining ingredients into the bowl and mix well.
2. Cover the bowl and place in the refrigerator for 2 hours.
3. Thread the marinated chicken onto the soaked skewers.
4. Insert a crisper plate in the Ninja Foodi air fryer baskets.
5. Place the chicken skewers in both baskets.
6. Select zone 1 then select "air fry" mode and set the temperature to 360 degrees F for 15 minutes. Press "match" to match zone 2 settings to zone 1. Press "start/stop" to begin.

Nutrition:

- (Per serving) Calories 526 | Fat 20.5g |Sodium 2210mg | Carbs 12.9g | Fiber 0.6g | Sugar 10g | Protein 69.7g

Broccoli Cheese Chicken

Servings: 4
Cooking Time: 25 Minutes
Ingredients:

- 1 tablespoon avocado oil
- 15 g chopped onion
- 35 g finely chopped broccoli
- 115 g cream cheese, at room temperature
- 60 g Cheddar cheese, shredded
- 1 teaspoon garlic powder
- ½ teaspoon sea salt, plus additional for seasoning, divided
- ¼ freshly ground black pepper, plus additional for seasoning, divided
- 900 g boneless, skinless chicken breasts
- 1 teaspoon smoked paprika

Directions:

1. Heat a medium skillet over medium-high heat and pour in the avocado oil. Add the onion and broccoli and cook, stirring occasionally, for 5 to 8 minutes, until the onion is tender.
2. Transfer to a large bowl and stir in the cream cheese, Cheddar cheese, and garlic powder, and season to taste with salt and pepper.
3. Hold a sharp knife parallel to the chicken breast and cut a long pocket into one side. Stuff the chicken pockets with the broccoli mixture, using toothpicks to secure the pockets around the filling.
4. In a small dish, combine the paprika, ½ teaspoon salt, and ¼ teaspoon pepper. Sprinkle this over the outside of the chicken.
5. Set the air fryer to 200ºC. Place the chicken in a single layer in the two air fryer drawers and cook for 14 to 16 minutes, until an instant-read thermometer reads 70ºC. Place the chicken on a plate and tent a piece of aluminum foil over the chicken. Allow to rest for 5 to 10 minutes before serving.

Cajun Chicken With Vegetables

Servings: 6

Cooking Time: 20 Minutes

Ingredients:

- 450g chicken breast, boneless & diced
- 1 tbsp Cajun seasoning
- 400g grape tomatoes
- ⅛ tsp dried thyme
- ⅛ tsp dried oregano
- 1 tsp smoked paprika
- 1 zucchini, diced
- 30ml olive oil
- 1 bell pepper, diced
- 1 tsp onion powder
- 1 ½ tsp garlic powder
- Pepper
- Salt

Directions:

1. In a bowl, toss chicken with vegetables, oil, herb, spices, and salt until well coated.
2. Insert a crisper plate in the Ninja Foodi air fryer baskets.
3. Add chicken and vegetable mixture to both baskets.
4. Select zone 1, then select "air fry" mode and set the temperature to 390 degrees F for 20 minutes. Press "match" to match zone 2 settings to zone 1. Press "start/stop" to begin.

Nutrition:

- (Per serving) Calories 153 | Fat 6.9g |Sodium 98mg | Carbs 6g | Fiber 1.6g | Sugar 3.5g | Protein 17.4g

Chicken Breast Strips

Servings:2

Cooking Time:22

Ingredients:

- 2 large organic egg
- 1-ounce buttermilk
- 1 cup of cornmeal
- ¼ cup all-purpose flour
- Salt and black pepper, to taste
- 1 pound of chicken breasts, cut into strips
- 2 tablespoons of oil bay seasoning
- oil spray, for greasing

Directions:

1. Take a medium bowl and whisk eggs with buttermilk.
2. In a separate large bowl mix flour, cornmeal, salt, black pepper, and oil bay seasoning.
3. First, dip the chicken breast strip in egg wash and then dredge into the flour mixture.
4. Coat the strip all over and layer on both the baskets that are already grease with oil spray.
5. Grease the chicken breast strips with oil spray as well.
6. Set the zone 1 basket to AIR FRY mode at 400 degrees F for 22 minutes.
7. Select the MATCH button for zone 2.
8. Hit the start button to let the cooking start.
9. Once the cooking cycle is done, serve.

Nutrition:

- (Per serving) Calories 788| Fat25g| Sodium835 mg | Carbs60g | Fiber 4.9g| Sugar1.5g | Protein79g

Lemon-pepper Chicken Thighs With Buttery Roasted Radishes

Servings: 4
Cooking Time: 28 Minutes
Ingredients:
- FOR THE CHICKEN
- 4 bone-in, skin-on chicken thighs (6 ounces each)
- 1 teaspoon olive oil
- 2 teaspoons lemon pepper
- ¼ teaspoon kosher salt
- FOR THE RADISHES
- 1 bunch radishes (greens removed), halved through the stem
- 1 teaspoon olive oil
- ¼ teaspoon kosher salt
- ¼ teaspoon freshly ground black pepper
- 1 tablespoon unsalted butter, cut into small pieces
- 2 tablespoons chopped fresh parsley

Directions:
1. To prep the chicken: Brush both sides of the chicken thighs with olive oil, then season with lemon pepper and salt.
2. To prep the radishes: In a large bowl, combine the radishes, olive oil, salt, and black pepper. Stir well to coat the radishes.
3. To cook the chicken and radishes: Install a crisper plate in each of the two baskets. Place the chicken skin-side up in the Zone 1 basket and insert the basket in the unit. Place the radishes in the Zone 2 basket and insert the basket in the unit.
4. Select Zone 1, select AIR FRY, set the temperature to 390°F, and set the time to 28 minutes.
5. Select Zone 2, select ROAST, set the temperature to 400°F, and set the time to 15 minutes. Select SMART FINISH.
6. Press START/PAUSE to begin cooking.
7. When the Zone 2 timer reads 5 minutes, press START/PAUSE. Remove the basket, scatter the butter pieces over the radishes, and reinsert the basket. Press START/PAUSE to resume cooking.
8. When cooking is complete, the chicken should be cooked through and the radishes will be soft. Stir the parsley into the radishes and serve.

Maple-mustard Glazed Turkey Tenderloin With Apple And Sage Stuffing

Servings: 4

Cooking Time: 35 Minutes

Ingredients:

- FOR THE TURKEY TENDERLOIN
- 2 tablespoons maple syrup
- 1 tablespoon unsalted butter, at room temperature
- 1 tablespoon Dijon mustard
- ½ teaspoon kosher salt
- ½ teaspoon freshly ground black pepper
- 1½ pounds turkey tenderloin
- FOR THE STUFFING
- 6 ounces seasoned stuffing mix
- 1½ cups chicken broth
- 1 apple, peeled, cored, and diced
- 1 tablespoon chopped fresh sage
- 2 teaspoons unsalted butter, cut into several pieces

Directions:

1. To prep the turkey tenderloin: In a small bowl, mix the maple syrup, butter, mustard, salt, and black pepper until smooth. Spread the maple mixture over the entire turkey tenderloin.

2. To prep the stuffing: In the Zone 2 basket, combine the stuffing mix and chicken broth. Stir well to ensure the bread is fully moistened. Stir in the apple and sage. Scatter the butter on top.

3. To cook the turkey and stuffing:

4. Install a crisper plate in the Zone 1 basket. Place the turkey tenderloin in the basket and insert the basket in the unit. Insert the Zone 2 basket in the unit.

5. Select Zone 1, select AIR FRY, set the temperature to 390°F, and set the time to 35 minutes.

6. Select Zone 2, select BAKE, set the temperature to 340°F, and set the time to 20 minutes. Select SMART FINISH.

7. Press START/PAUSE to begin cooking.

8. When the Zone 2 timer reads 10 minutes, press START/PAUSE. Remove the basket and stir the stuffing. Reinsert the basket and press START/PAUSE to resume cooking.

9. When cooking is complete, the turkey will be cooked through and the stuffing will have absorbed all the liquid and be slightly crisp on top. Serve warm.

Sweet-and-sour Chicken With Pineapple Cauliflower Rice

Servings: 4
Cooking Time: 30 Minutes
Ingredients:

- FOR THE CHICKEN
- ¼ cup cornstarch, plus 2 teaspoons
- ¼ teaspoon kosher salt
- 2 large eggs
- 1 tablespoon sesame oil
- 1½ pounds boneless, skinless chicken breasts, cut into 1-inch pieces
- Nonstick cooking spray
- 6 tablespoons ketchup
- ¾ cup apple cider vinegar
- 1½ tablespoons soy sauce
- 1 tablespoon sugar
- FOR THE CAULIFLOWER RICE
- 1 cup finely diced fresh pineapple
- 1 red bell pepper, thinly sliced
- 1 small red onion, thinly sliced
- 1 tablespoon vegetable oil
- 2 cups frozen cauliflower rice, thawed
- 2 tablespoons soy sauce
- 1 teaspoon sesame oil
- 2 scallions, sliced

Directions:

1. To prep the chicken:
2. Set up a breading station with two small shallow bowls. Combine ¼ cup of cornstarch and the salt in the first bowl. In the second bowl, beat the eggs with the sesame oil.
3. Dip the chicken pieces in the cornstarch mixture to coat, then into the egg mixture, then back into the cornstarch mixture to coat. Mist the coated pieces with cooking spray.
4. In a small bowl, whisk together the ketchup, vinegar, soy sauce, sugar, and remaining 2 teaspoons of cornstarch.
5. To prep the cauliflower rice: Blot the pineapple dry with a paper towel. In a large bowl, combine the pineapple, bell pepper, onion, and vegetable oil.
6. To cook the chicken and cauliflower rice: Install a crisper plate in each of the two baskets. Place the chicken in the Zone 1 basket and insert the basket in the unit. Place a piece of aluminum foil over the crisper plate in the Zone 2 basket and add the pineapple mixture. Insert the basket in the unit.
7. Select Zone 1, select AIR FRY, set the temperature to 400°F, and set the time to 30 minutes.
8. Select Zone 2, select AIR BROIL, set the temperature to 450°F, and set the time to 12 minutes. Select SMART FINISH.
9. Press START/PAUSE to begin cooking.
10. When the Zone 2 timer reads 4 minutes, press START/PAUSE. Remove the basket and stir in the cauliflower rice, soy sauce, and sesame oil. Reinsert the basket and press START/PAUSE to resume cooking.
11. When cooking is complete, the chicken will be golden brown and cooked through and the rice warmed through. Stir the scallions into the rice and serve.

Crispy Dill Chicken Strips

Servings: 4

Cooking Time: 10 Minutes

Ingredients:

- 2 whole boneless, skinless chicken breasts (about 450 g each), halved lengthwise
- 230 ml Italian dressing
- 110 g finely crushed crisps
- 1 tablespoon dried dill weed
- 1 tablespoon garlic powder
- 1 large egg, beaten
- 1 to 2 tablespoons oil

Directions:

1. In a large resealable bag, combine the chicken and Italian dressing. Seal the bag and refrigerate to marinate at least 1 hour.
2. In a shallow dish, stir together the potato chips, dill, and garlic powder. Place the beaten egg in a second shallow dish.
3. Remove the chicken from the marinade. Roll the chicken pieces in the egg and the crisp mixture, coating thoroughly.
4. Preheat the air fryer to 170°C. Line the two air fryer drawers with parchment paper.
5. Place the coated chicken on the parchment and spritz with oil.
6. Cook for 5 minutes. Flip the chicken, spritz it with oil, and cook for 5 minutes more until the outsides are crispy and the insides are no longer pink.

Chicken Wings

Servings:3

Cooking Time:20

Ingredients:

- 1 cup chicken batter mix, Louisiana
- 9 Chicken wings
- ½ teaspoon of smoked paprika
- 2 tablespoons of Dijon mustard
- 1 tablespoon of cayenne pepper
- 1 teaspoon of meat tenderizer, powder
- oil spray, for greasing

Directions:

1. Pat dry chicken wings and add mustard, paprika, meat tenderizer, and cayenne pepper.
2. Dredge it in the chicken batter mix.
3. Oil sprays the chicken wings.
4. Grease both baskets of the air fryer.
5. Divide the wings between the two zones of the air fryer.
6. Set zone 1 to AR FRY mode at 400 degrees F for 20 minutes
7. Select MATCH for zone 2.
8. Hit start to begin with the cooking.
9. Once the cooking cycle complete, serve, and enjoy hot.

Nutrition:

- (Per serving) Calories621 | Fat 32.6g| Sodium 2016mg | Carbs 46.6g | Fiber 1.1g | Sugar 0.2g | Protein 32.1g

Chicken Tenders And Curly Fries

Servings: 4
Cooking Time: 35 Minutes
Ingredients:

- 1-pound frozen chicken tenders
- 1-pound frozen curly French fries
- Dipping sauces of your choice

Directions:

1. Place a crisper plate in each drawer. In the zone 1 drawer, place the chicken tenders, then place the drawer into the unit.
2. Fill the zone 2 drawer with the curly French fries, then place the drawer in the unit.
3. Select zone 1, then AIR FRY, and set the temperature to 390 degrees F/ 200 degrees C with a 22-minute timer. Select zone 2, then AIR FRY, and set the temperature to 400 degrees F/ 200 degrees C with a 30-minute timer. Select SYNC. To begin cooking, press the START/STOP button.
4. Press START/STOP to pause the device when the zone 1 and 2 times reach 8 minutes. Shake the drawers for 10 seconds after removing them from the unit. To resume cooking, re-insert the drawers into the unit and press START/STOP.
5. Enjoy!

Nutrition:

- (Per serving) Calories 500 | Fat 19.8g | Sodium 680mg | Carbs 50.1g | Fiber 4.1g | Sugar 0g | Protein 27.9g

Beef, Pork, And Lamb Recipes
Mozzarella Stuffed Beef And Pork Meatballs

Servings: 4 To 6
Cooking Time: 12 Minutes
Ingredients:

- 1 tablespoon olive oil
- 1 small onion, finely chopped
- 1 to 2 cloves garlic, minced
- 340 g beef mince
- 340 g pork mince
- 180 ml bread crumbs
- 60 ml grated Parmesan cheese
- 60 ml finely chopped fresh parsley
- ½ teaspoon dried oregano
- 1½ teaspoons salt
- Freshly ground black pepper, to taste
- 2 eggs, lightly beaten
- 140 g low-moisture Mozzarella or other melting cheese, cut into 1-inch cubes

Directions:

1. Preheat a skillet over medium-high heat. Add the oil and cook the onion and garlic until tender, but not browned. 2. Transfer the onion and garlic to a large bowl and add the beef, pork, bread crumbs, Parmesan cheese, parsley, oregano, salt, pepper and eggs. Mix well until all the ingredients are combined. Divide the mixture into 12 evenly sized balls. Make one meatball at a time, by pressing a hole in the meatball mixture with the finger and pushing a piece of Mozzarella cheese into the hole. Mold the meat back into a ball, enclosing the cheese. 3. Preheat the air fryer to 192ºC. 4. Transfer meatballs to the two air fryer drawers and air fry for 12 minutes, shaking the drawers and turning the meatballs twice during the cooking process. Serve warm.

Barbecue Ribs With Roasted Green Beans And Shallots

Servings:4
Cooking Time: 40 Minutes
Ingredients:

- FOR THE RIBS
- 1 tablespoon light brown sugar
- 1 tablespoon smoked paprika
- 1 tablespoon chili powder
- 2 teaspoons kosher salt
- 1 teaspoon freshly ground black pepper
- 1 teaspoon garlic powder
- ¼ teaspoon cayenne pepper (optional)
- 2 pounds pork ribs
- 1 cup barbecue sauce (your favorite), for serving
- FOR THE GREEN BEANS AND SHALLOTS
- 1 pound green beans, trimmed
- 2 shallots, sliced
- 1 tablespoon olive oil
- ¼ teaspoon kosher salt

Directions:

1. To prep the ribs: In a small bowl, combine the brown sugar, paprika, chili powder, salt, black pepper, garlic powder, and cayenne (if using).
2. Rub the spice blend all over both sides of the ribs.
3. To prep the green beans and shallots: In a large bowl, combine the green beans, shallots, and oil. Toss to coat. Season with the salt.
4. To cook the ribs and vegetables: Install a crisper plate in each of the two baskets. Place the ribs in the Zone 1 basket and insert the basket in the unit. Place the green beans in the Zone 2 basket and insert the basket in the unit.
5. Select Zone 1, select AIR FRY, set the temperature to 375°F, and set the time to 40 minutes.
6. Select Zone 2, select ROAST, set the temperature to 400°F, and set the time to 20 minutes. Select SMART FINISH.
7. Press START/PAUSE to begin cooking.
8. When the Zone 1 timer reads 10 minutes, press START/PAUSE. Increase the temperature of Zone 1 to 400°F. Press START/PAUSE to resume cooking.
9. When cooking is complete, an instant-read thermometer inserted into the ribs should read 170°F and the green beans should be tender-crisp. Serve topped with your favorite barbecue sauce.

Nutrition:

- (Per serving) Calories: 541; Total fat: 27g; Saturated fat: 9g; Carbohydrates: 48g; Fiber: 4.5g; Protein: 28g; Sodium: 1,291mg

Garlic Butter Steak Bites

Servings: 3
Cooking Time: 16 Minutes
Ingredients:
- Oil, for spraying
- 450 g boneless steak, cut into 1-inch pieces
- 2 tablespoons olive oil
- 1 teaspoon Worcestershire sauce
- ½ teaspoon granulated garlic
- ½ teaspoon salt
- ¼ teaspoon freshly ground black pepper

Directions:
1. Preheat the air fryer to 204ºC. Line the two air fryer drawers with parchment and spray lightly with oil.
2. In a medium bowl, combine the steak, olive oil, Worcestershire sauce, garlic, salt, and black pepper and toss until evenly coated.
3. Place the steak in a single layer in the two prepared drawers.
4. Cook for 10 to 16 minutes, flipping every 3 to 4 minutes. The total cooking time will depend on the thickness of the meat and your preferred doneness. If you want it well done, it may take up to 5 additional minutes.

Minute Steak Roll-ups

Servings: 4
Cooking Time: 8 To 10 Minutes
Ingredients:
- 4 minute steaks (170 g each)
- 1 (450 g) bottle Italian dressing
- 1 teaspoon salt
- ½ teaspoon freshly ground black pepper
- 120 ml finely chopped brown onion
- 120 ml finely chopped green pepper
- 120 ml finely chopped mushrooms
- 1 to 2 tablespoons oil

Directions:
1. In a large resealable bag or airtight storage container, combine the steaks and Italian dressing. Seal the bag and refrigerate to marinate for 2 hours.
2. Remove the steaks from the marinade and place them on a cutting board. Discard the marinade. Evenly season the steaks with salt and pepper.
3. In a small bowl, stir together the onion, pepper, and mushrooms. Sprinkle the onion mixture evenly over the steaks. Roll up the steaks, jelly roll-style, and secure with toothpicks.
4. Preheat the air fryer to 204ºC.
5. Place the steaks in the two air fryer drawers.
6. Cook for 4 minutes. Flip the steaks and spritz them with oil. Cook for 4 to 6 minutes more until the internal temperature reaches 64ºC. Let rest for 5 minutes before serving.

Balsamic Steak Tips With Roasted Asparagus And Mushroom Medley

Servings:4

Cooking Time: 25 Minutes

Ingredients:

- FOR THE STEAK TIPS
- 1½ pounds sirloin tips
- ½ cup olive oil
- ¼ cup balsamic vinegar
- ¼ cup packed light brown sugar
- 1 tablespoon reduced-sodium soy sauce
- 1 teaspoon finely chopped fresh rosemary
- 1 teaspoon minced garlic
- FOR THE ASPARAGUS AND MUSHROOMS
- 6 ounces sliced cremini mushrooms
- 1 small red onion, sliced
- 1 tablespoon olive oil
- 1 pound asparagus, tough ends trimmed
- ⅛ teaspoon kosher salt

Directions:

1. To prep the steak tips: In a large bowl, combine the sirloin tips, oil, vinegar, brown sugar, soy sauce, rosemary, and garlic. Mix well to coat the steak.

2. To prep the mushrooms: In a large bowl, combine the mushrooms, onion, and oil.

3. To cook the steak and vegetables: Install a crisper plate in each of the two baskets. Shake any excess marinade from the steak tips, place the steak in the Zone 1 basket, and insert the basket in the unit. Place the mushrooms and onions in the Zone 2 basket and insert the basket in the unit.

4. Select Zone 1, select AIR FRY, set the temperature to 400°F, and set the time to 12 minutes.

5. Select Zone 2, select ROAST, set the temperature to 400°F, and set the time to 25 minutes. Select SMART FINISH.

6. Press START/PAUSE to begin cooking.

7. When the Zone 2 timer reads 10 minutes, press START/PAUSE. Remove the basket, add the asparagus to the mushrooms and onion, and sprinkle with salt. Reinsert the basket and press START/PAUSE to resume cooking.

8. When cooking is complete, the beef should be cooked to your liking and the asparagus crisp-tender. Serve warm.

Nutrition:

- (Per serving) Calories: 524; Total fat: 33g; Saturated fat: 2.5g; Carbohydrates: 16g; Fiber: 3g; Protein: 41g; Sodium: 192mg

Spicy Lamb Chops

Servings:4
Cooking Time:15
Ingredients:

- 12 lamb chops, bone-in
- Salt and black pepper, to taste
- ½ teaspoon of lemon zest
- 1 tablespoon of lemon juice
- 1 teaspoon of paprika
- 1 teaspoon of garlic powder
- ½ teaspoon of Italian seasoning
- ¼ teaspoon of onion powder

Directions:

1. Add the lamb chops to the bowl and sprinkle salt, garlic powder, Italian seasoning, onion powder, black pepper, lemon zest, lemon juice, and paprika.
2. Rub the chops well, and divide it between both the baskets of the air fryer.
3. Set zone 1 basket to 400 degrees F, for 15 minutes at AIR FRY mode.
4. Select MATCH for zone2 basket.
5. After 10 minutes, take out the baskets and flip the chops cook for the remaining minutes, and then serve.

Nutrition:

- (Per serving) Calories 787| Fat 45.3g| Sodium1 mg | Carbs 16.1g | Fiber0.3g | Sugar 0.4g | Protein 75.3g

Honey-baked Pork Loin

Servings: 6
Cooking Time: 22 To 25 Minutes
Ingredients:

- 60 ml honey
- 60 ml freshly squeezed lemon juice
- 2 tablespoons soy sauce
- 1 teaspoon garlic powder
- 1 (900 g) pork loin
- 2 tablespoons vegetable oil

Directions:

1. In a medium bowl, whisk together the honey, lemon juice, soy sauce, and garlic powder. Reserve half of the mixture for basting during cooking.
2. Cut 5 slits in the pork loin and transfer it to a resealable bag. Add the remaining honey mixture. Seal the bag and refrigerate to marinate for at least 2 hours.
3. Preheat the air fryer to 204°C. Line the two air fryer drawers with parchment paper.
4. Remove the pork from the marinade, and place it on the parchment. Spritz with oil, then baste with the reserved marinade.
5. Cook for 15 minutes. Flip the pork, baste with more marinade and spritz with oil again. Cook for 7 to 10 minutes more until the internal temperature reaches 64°C. Let rest for 5 minutes before serving.

Seasoned Lamb Steak

Servings: 2
Cooking Time: 10 Minutes
Ingredients:

- 2 lamb steaks
- ½ teaspoon kosher salt
- Drizzle of olive oil
- ½ teaspoon ground black pepper

Directions:

1. Take a bowl, add every ingredient except lamb steak. Mix well.
2. Rub lamb steaks with a little olive oil.
3. Press each side of steak into salt and pepper mixture.
4. Grease each basket of "Zone 1" and "Zone 2" of Ninja Foodi 2-Basket Air Fryer.
5. Press "Zone 1" and "Zone 2" and then rotate the knob for each zone to select "Air Fry".
6. Set the heat to 400 degrees F/ 200 degrees C for both zones and then set the time for 5 minutes to preheat.
7. After preheating, arrange steak into the basket of each zone.
8. Slide each basket into Air Fryer and set the time for 5 minutes.
9. While cooking, flip the steak once halfway through and cook for more 5 minutes.
10. After cooking time is completed, remove it from Air Fryer and place onto a platter for about 10 minutes before slicing.
11. With a sharp knife, cut each steak into desired-sized slices and serve.

Chorizo And Beef Burger

Servings: 4
Cooking Time: 15 Minutes
Ingredients:

- 340 g 80/20 beef mince
- 110 g Mexican-style chorizo crumb
- 60 ml chopped onion
- 5 slices pickled jalapeños, chopped
- 2 teaspoons chili powder
- 1 teaspoon minced garlic
- ¼ teaspoon cumin

Directions:

1. In a large bowl, mix all ingredients. Divide the mixture into four sections and form them into burger patties.
2. Place burger patties into the two air fryer drawers.
3. Adjust the temperature to 192ºC and air fry for 15 minutes.
4. Flip the patties halfway through the cooking time. Serve warm.

Bell Peppers With Sausages

Servings:4
Cooking Time:20
Ingredients:

- 6 beef or pork Italian sausages
- 4 bell peppers, whole
- Oil spray, for greasing
- 2 cups of cooked rice
- 1 cup of sour cream

Directions:

1. Put the bell pepper in the zone 1 basket and sausages in the zone 2 basket of the air fryer.
2. Set zone 1 to AIR FRY MODE for 10 minutes at 400 degrees F.
3. For zone 2 set it to 20 minutes at 375 degrees F.
4. Hit the smart finish button, so both finish at the same time.
5. After 5 minutes take out the sausage basket and break or mince it with a plastic spatula.
6. Then, let the cooking cycle finish.
7. Once done serve the minced meat with bell peppers and serve over cooked rice with a dollop of sour cream.

Nutrition:

- (Per serving) Calories1356 | Fat 81.2g| Sodium 3044 mg | Carbs 96g | Fiber 3.1g | Sugar 8.3g | Protein 57.2 g

Filet Mignon Wrapped In Bacon

Servings: 2
Cooking Time: 20 Minutes
Ingredients:

- 2 (2-ounce) filet mignon
- 2 bacon slices
- Olive oil cooking spray
- Salt and ground black pepper, as required

Directions:

1. Wrap 1 bacon slice around each filet mignon and secure with toothpicks.
2. Season the filets with salt and black pepper lightly.
3. Grease each basket of "Zone 1" and "Zone 2" of Ninja Foodi 2-Basket Air Fryer.
4. Press "Zone 1" and "Zone 2" and then rotate the knob for each zone to select "Air Fry".
5. Set the temperature to 400 degrees F/ 200 degrees C for both zones and then set the time for 5 minutes to preheat.
6. After preheating, arrange the filets into the basket of each zone.
7. Slide each basket into Air Fryer and set the time for 15 minutes.
8. While cooking, flip the filets once halfway through.
9. After cooking time is completed, remove the filets from Air Fryer and serve hot.

Rosemary Ribeye Steaks And Mongolian-style Beef

Servings: 6

Cooking Time: 15 Minutes

Ingredients:

- Rosemary Ribeye Steaks:
- 60 ml butter
- 1 clove garlic, minced
- Salt and ground black pepper, to taste
- 1½ tablespoons balsamic vinegar
- 60 ml rosemary, chopped
- 2 ribeye steaks
- Mongolian-Style Beef:
- Oil, for spraying
- 60 ml cornflour
- 450 g bavette or skirt steak, thinly sliced
- 180 ml packed light brown sugar
- 120 ml soy sauce
- 2 teaspoons toasted sesame oil
- 1 tablespoon minced garlic
- ½ teaspoon ground ginger
- 120 ml water
- Cooked white rice or ramen noodles, for serving

Directions:

1. Make the Rosemary Ribeye Steaks :
2. Melt the butter in a skillet over medium heat. Add the garlic and fry until fragrant.
3. Remove the skillet from the heat and add the salt, pepper, and vinegar. Allow it to cool.
4. Add the rosemary, then pour the mixture into a Ziploc bag.
5. Put the ribeye steaks in the bag and shake well, coating the meat well. Refrigerate for an hour, then allow to sit for a further twenty minutes.
6. Preheat the zone 1 air fryer drawer to 204ºC.
7. Air fry the ribeye steaks for 15 minutes.
8. Take care when removing the steaks from the air fryer and plate up.
9. Serve immediately.
10. Make the Mongolian-Style Beef :
11. Line the zone 2 air fryer drawer with parchment and spray lightly with oil.
12. Place the cornflour in a bowl and dredge the steak until evenly coated. Shake off any excess cornflour.
13. Place the steak in the prepared drawer and spray lightly with oil.
14. Roast at 200ºC for 5 minutes, flip, and cook for another 5 minutes.
15. In a small saucepan, combine the brown sugar, soy sauce, sesame oil, garlic, ginger, and water and bring to a boil over medium-high heat, stirring frequently. Remove from the heat.
16. Transfer the meat to the sauce and toss until evenly coated. Let sit for about 5 minutes so the steak absorbs the flavors. Serve with white rice or ramen noodles.

Beef Ribs Ii

Servings:2
Cooking Time:1
Ingredients:

- ¼ cup olive oil
- 4 garlic cloves, minced
- ½ cup white wine vinegar
- ¼ cup soy sauce, reduced-sodium
- ¼ cup Worcestershire sauce
- 1 lemon juice
- Salt and black pepper, to taste
- 2 tablespoons of Italian seasoning
- 1 teaspoon of smoked paprika
- 2 tablespoons of mustard
- ½ cup maple syrup
- Meat Ingredients:
- Oil spray, for greasing
- 8 beef ribs lean

Directions:

1. Take a large bowl and add all the ingredients under marinade ingredients.
2. Put the marinade in a zip lock bag and add ribs to it.
3. Let it sit for 4 hours.
4. Now take out the basket of air fryer and grease the baskets with oil spray.
5. Now dived the ribs among two baskets.
6. Set it to AIR fry mode at 220 degrees F for 30 minutes.
7. Select Pause and take out the baskets.
8. Afterward, flip the ribs and cook for 30 minutes at 250 degrees F.
9. Once done, serve the juicy and tender ribs.
10. Enjoy.

Nutrition:

- (Per serving) Calories 1927| Fat116g| Sodium 1394mg | Carbs 35.2g | Fiber 1.3g| Sugar29 g | Protein 172.3g

Glazed Steak Recipe

Servings:2
Cooking Time:25
Ingredients:

- 1 pound of beef steaks
- ½ cup, soy sauce
- Salt and black pepper, to taste
- 1 tablespoon of vegetable oil
- 1 teaspoon of grated ginger
- 4 cloves garlic, minced
- 1/4 cup brown sugar

Directions:

1. Take a bowl and whisk together soy sauce, salt, pepper, vegetable oil, garlic, brown sugar, and ginger.
2. Once a paste is made rub the steak with the marinate
3. Let it sit for 30 minutes.
4. After 30 minutes add the steak to the air fryer basket and set it to AIR BROIL mode at 400 degrees F for 18-22 minutes.
5. After 10 minutes, hit pause and takeout the basket.
6. Let the steak flip and again let it AIR BROIL for the remaining minutes.
7. Once 25 minutes of cooking cycle completes.
8. Take out the steak and let it rest. Serve by cutting into slices.
9. Enjoy.

Nutrition:

- (Per serving) Calories 563| Fat 21 g| Sodium 156mg | Carbs 20.6g | Fiber0.3 g| Sugar17.8 g | Protein69.4 g

Taco Seasoned Steak

Servings: 6
Cooking Time: 30 Minutes
Ingredients:

- 1 (1-pound) flank steaks
- 1½ tablespoons taco seasoning rub

Directions:

1. Grease each basket of "Zone 1" and "Zone 2" of Ninja Foodi 2-Basket Air Fryer.
2. Press "Zone 1" and "Zone 2" and then rotate the knob for each zone to select "Bake".
3. Set the temperature to 420 degrees F/ 215 degrees C for both zones and then set the time for 5 minutes to preheat.
4. Rub the steaks with taco seasoning evenly.
5. After preheating, arrange the steak into the basket of each zone.
6. Slide each basket into Air Fryer and set the time for 30 minutes.
7. After cooking time is completed, remove the steaks from Air Fryer and place onto a cutting board for about 10-15 minutes before slicing.
8. With a sharp knife, cut each steak into desired size slices and serve.

Honey Glazed Bbq Pork Ribs

Servings: 4
Cooking Time: 30 Minutes
Ingredients:

- 2 pounds pork ribs
- ¼ cup honey, divided
- 1 cup BBQ sauce
- ½ teaspoon garlic powder
- 2 tablespoons tomato ketchup
- 1 tablespoon Worcestershire sauce
- 1 tablespoon low-sodium soy sauce
- Freshly ground white pepper, as required

Directions:

1. In a bowl, mix together honey and the remaining ingredients except pork ribs.
2. Add the pork ribs and coat with the mixture generously.
3. Refrigerate to marinate for about 20 minutes.
4. Grease each basket of "Zone 1" and "Zone 2" of Ninja Foodi 2-Basket Air Fryer.
5. Press "Zone 1" and "Zone 2" and then rotate the knob for each zone to select "Air Fry".
6. Set the temperature to 355 degrees F/ 180 degrees C for both zones and then set the time for 5 minutes to preheat.
7. After preheating, arrange the ribs into the basket of each zone.
8. Slide each basket into Air Fryer and set the time for 26 minutes.
9. While cooking, flip the ribs once halfway through.
10. After cooking time is completed, remove the ribs from Air Fryer and place onto serving plates.
11. Drizzle with the remaining honey and serve immediately.

Blue Cheese Steak Salad

Servings: 4
Cooking Time: 22 Minutes
Ingredients:

- 2 tablespoons balsamic vinegar
- 2 tablespoons red wine vinegar
- 1 tablespoon Dijon mustard
- 1 tablespoon granulated sweetener
- 1 teaspoon minced garlic
- Sea salt and freshly ground black pepper, to taste
- 180 ml extra-virgin olive oil
- 450 g boneless rump steak
- Avocado oil spray
- 1 small red onion, cut into ¼-inch-thick rounds
- 170 g baby spinach
- 120 ml cherry tomatoes, halved
- 85 g blue cheese, crumbled

Directions:

1. In a blender, combine the balsamic vinegar, red wine vinegar, Dijon mustard, sweetener, and garlic. Season with salt and pepper and process until smooth. With the blender running, drizzle in the olive oil. Process until well combined. Transfer to a jar with a tight-fitting lid, and refrigerate until ready to serve .
2. Season the steak with salt and pepper and let sit at room temperature for at least 45 minutes, time permitting.
3. Set the zone 1 air fryer drawer to 204ºC. Spray the steak with oil and place it in the zone 1 air fryer drawer. Spray the onion slices with oil and place them in the zone 2 air fryer drawer.
4. In zone 1, air fry for 6 minutes. Flip the steak and spray it with more oil. Air fry for 6 minutes more for medium-rare or until the steak is done to your liking.
5. In zone 2, cook at 204ºC for 5 minutes. Flip the onion slices and spray them with more oil. Air fry for 5 minutes more.
6. Transfer the steak to a plate, tent with a piece of aluminum foil, and allow it to rest. Slice the steak diagonally into thin strips. Place the spinach, cherry tomatoes, onion slices, and steak in a large bowl. Toss with the desired amount of dressing. Sprinkle with crumbled blue cheese and serve.

Parmesan Pork Chops

Servings: 4
Cooking Time: 15 Minutes.
Ingredients:

- 4 boneless pork chops
- 2 tablespoons olive oil
- ½ cup freshly grated Parmesan
- 1 teaspoon salt

- 1 teaspoon paprika
- 1 teaspoon garlic powder
- 1 teaspoon onion powder
- ½ teaspoon black pepper

Directions:

1. Pat dry the pork chops with a paper towel and rub them with olive oil.
2. Mix parmesan with spices in a medium bowl.
3. Rub the pork chops with Parmesan mixture.
4. Place 2 seasoned pork chops in each of the two crisper plate
5. Return the crisper plate to the Ninja Foodi Dual Zone Air Fryer.
6. Choose the Air Fry mode for Zone 1 and set the temperature to 390 degrees F and the time to 15 minutes.
7. Select the "MATCH" button to copy the settings for Zone 2.
8. Initiate cooking by pressing the START/STOP button.
9. Flip the pork chops when cooked halfway through, then resume cooking.
10. Serve warm.

Nutrition:

- (Per serving) Calories 396 | Fat 23.2g |Sodium 622mg | Carbs 0.7g | Fiber 0g | Sugar 0g | Protein 45.6g

Bacon-wrapped Filet Mignon

Servings: 4
Cooking Time: 15 Minutes
Ingredients:

- 4 bacon slices
- 4 (4-ounce) filet mignon
- Salt and ground black pepper, as required
- Olive oil cooking spray

Directions:

1. Wrap 1 bacon slice around each filet mignon and secure with toothpicks.
2. Spray the filet mignon with cooking spray evenly. Season the filets with salt and black pepper lightly.
3. Grease each basket of "Zone 1" and "Zone 2" of Ninja Foodi 2-Basket Air Fryer.
4. Press "Zone 1" and "Zone 2" and then rotate the knob for each zone to select "Air Fry".
5. Set the temperature to 400 degrees F/ 200 degrees C for both zones and then set the time for 5 minutes to preheat.
6. After preheating, arrange 2 filets into the basket of each zone.
7. Slide each basket into Air Fryer and set the time for 15 minutes.
8. While cooking, flip the filets once halfway through.
9. After cooking time is completed, remove the filets from Air Fryer and serve hot.

Fish And Seafood Recipes
<u>Shrimp Po'boys With Sweet Potato Fries</u>

Servings:4
Cooking Time: 30 Minutes
Ingredients:
- FOR THE SHRIMP PO'BOYS
- ½ cup buttermilk
- 1 tablespoon Louisiana-style hot sauce
- ¾ cup all-purpose flour
- ½ cup cornmeal
- ½ teaspoon kosher salt
- ½ teaspoon paprika
- ½ teaspoon garlic powder
- ½ teaspoon freshly ground black pepper
- 1 pound peeled medium shrimp, thawed if frozen
- Nonstock cooking spray
- ½ cup store-bought rémoulade sauce
- 4 French bread rolls, halved lengthwise
- ½ cup shredded lettuce
- 1 tomato, sliced
- FOR THE SWEET POTATO FRIES
- 2 medium sweet potatoes
- 2 teaspoons vegetable oil
- ¼ teaspoon garlic powder
- ¼ teaspoon paprika
- ¼ teaspoon kosher salt

Directions:
1. To prep the shrimp: In a medium bowl, combine the buttermilk and hot sauce. In a shallow bowl, combine the flour, cornmeal, salt, paprika, garlic powder, and black pepper.
2. Add the shrimp to the buttermilk and stir to coat. Remove the shrimp, letting the excess buttermilk drip off, then add to the cornmeal mixture to coat.
3. Spritz the breaded shrimp with cooking spray, then let sit for 10 minutes.
4. To prep the sweet potatoes: Peel the sweet potatoes and cut them lengthwise into ¼-inch-thick sticks (like shoestring fries).
5. In a large bowl, combine the sweet potatoes, oil, garlic powder, paprika, and salt. Toss to coat.
6. To cook the shrimp and fries: Install a crisper plate in each of the two baskets. Place the shrimp in the Zone 1 basket and insert the basket in the unit. Place the sweet potatoes in a single layer in the Zone 2 basket and insert the basket in the unit.
7. Select Zone 1, select AIR FRY, set the temperature to 390°F, and set the timer to 13 minutes.
8. Select Zone 2, select AIR FRY, set the temperature to 400°F, and set the timer to 30 minutes. Select SMART FINISH.
9. Press START/PAUSE to begin cooking.
10. When cooking is complete, the shrimp should be golden and cooked through and the sweet potato fries crisp.
11. Spread the rémoulade on the cut sides of the rolls. Divide the lettuce and tomato among the rolls, then top with the fried shrimp. Serve with the sweet potato fries on the side.
Nutrition:
- (Per serving) Calories: 669; Total fat: 22g; Saturated fat: 2g; Carbohydrates: 86g; Fiber: 3.5g; Protein: 33g; Sodium: 1,020mg

Parmesan Fish Fillets

Servings: 4
Cooking Time: 17 Minutes
Ingredients:

- 50 g grated Parmesan cheese
- ½ teaspoon fennel seed
- ½ teaspoon tarragon
- ⅓ teaspoon mixed peppercorns
- 2 eggs, beaten
- 4 (110 g) fish fillets, halved
- 2 tablespoons dry white wine
- 1 teaspoon seasoned salt

Directions:

1. Preheat the air fryer to 175ºC.
2. Place the grated Parmesan cheese, fennel seed, tarragon, and mixed peppercorns in a food processor and pulse for about 20 seconds until well combined. Transfer the cheese mixture to a shallow dish.
3. Place the beaten eggs in another shallow dish.
4. Drizzle the dry white wine over the top of fish fillets. Dredge each fillet in the beaten eggs on both sides, shaking off any excess, then roll them in the cheese mixture until fully coated. Season with the salt.
5. Arrange the fillets in the two air fryer baskets and air fry for about 17 minutes, or until the fish is cooked through and no longer translucent. Flip the fillets once halfway through the cooking time.
6. Cool for 5 minutes before serving.

South Indian Fried Fish

Servings: 4
Cooking Time: 8 Minutes
Ingredients:

- 2 tablespoons olive oil
- 2 tablespoons fresh lime or lemon juice
- 1 teaspoon minced fresh ginger
- 1 clove garlic, minced
- 1 teaspoon ground turmeric
- ½ teaspoon kosher or coarse sea salt
- ¼ to ½ teaspoon cayenne pepper
- 455 g tilapia fillets (2 to 3 fillets)
- Olive oil spray
- Lime or lemon wedges (optional)

Directions:

1. In a large bowl, combine the oil, lime juice, ginger, garlic, turmeric, salt, and cayenne. Stir until well combined; set aside.
2. Cut each tilapia fillet into three or four equal-size pieces. Add the fish to the bowl and gently mix until all of the fish is coated in the marinade. Marinate for 10 to 15 minutes at room temperature.
3. Spray the air fryer basket with olive oil spray. Place the fish in the basket and spray the fish. Set the air fryer to 165ºC for 3 minutes to partially cook the fish. Set the air fryer to 205ºC for 5 minutes to finish cooking and crisp up the fish.
4. Carefully remove the fish from the basket. Serve hot, with lemon wedges if desired.

Nutty Prawns With Amaretto Glaze

Servings: 10 To 12
Cooking Time: 10 Minutes

Ingredients:

- 120 g plain flour
- ½ teaspoon baking powder
- 1 teaspoon salt
- 2 eggs, beaten
- 120 ml milk
- 2 tablespoons olive or vegetable oil
- 185 g sliced almonds
- 900 g large prawns (about 32 to 40 prawns), peeled and deveined, tails left on
- 470 ml amaretto liqueur

Directions:

1. Combine the flour, baking powder and salt in a large bowl. Add the eggs, milk and oil and stir until it forms a smooth batter. Coarsely crush the sliced almonds into a second shallow dish with your hands.
2. Dry the prawns well with paper towels. Dip the prawns into the batter and shake off any excess batter, leaving just enough to lightly coat the prawns. Transfer the prawns to the dish with the almonds and coat completely. Place the coated prawns on a plate or baking sheet and when all the prawns have been coated, freeze the prawns for an 1 hour, or as long as a week before air frying.
3. Preheat the air fryer to 204°C.
4. Transfer frozen prawns to the two air fryer drawers. Air fry for 6 minutes. Turn the prawns over and air fry for an additional 4 minutes.
5. While the prawns are cooking, bring the Amaretto to a boil in a small saucepan on the stovetop. Lower the heat and simmer until it has reduced and thickened into a glaze, about 10 minutes.
6. Remove the prawns from the air fryer and brush both sides with the warm amaretto glaze. Serve warm.

Salmon With Fennel Salad

Servings: 4
Cooking Time: 17 Minutes

Ingredients:

- 2 teaspoons fresh parsley, chopped
- 1 teaspoon fresh thyme, chopped
- 1 teaspoon salt
- 4 (6-oz) skinless center-cut salmon fillets
- 2 tablespoons olive oil
- 4 cups fennel, sliced
- ⅔ cup Greek yogurt
- 1 garlic clove, grated
- 2 tablespoons orange juice
- 1 teaspoon lemon juice
- 2 tablespoons fresh dill, chopped

Directions:

1. Preheat your Ninja Foodi Dual Zone Air Fryer to 200 degrees F.
2. Mix ½ teaspoon of salt, thyme, and parsley in a small bowl.
3. Brush the salmon with oil first, then rub liberally rub the herb mixture.
4. Place 2 salmon fillets in each of the crisper plate.
5. Return the crisper plate to the Ninja Foodi Dual Zone Air Fryer.
6. Choose the Air Fry mode for Zone 1 and set the temperature to 390 degrees F and the time to 17 minutes|
7. Select the "MATCH" button to copy the settings for Zone 2.
8. Initiate cooking by pressing the START/STOP button.
9. Meanwhile, mix fennel with garlic, yogurt, lemon juice, orange juice, remaining salt, and dill in a mixing bowl.
10. Serve the air fried salmon fillets with fennel salad.
11. Enjoy.

Lemon-pepper Trout

Servings: 4
Cooking Time: 15 Minutes
Ingredients:

- 4 trout fillets
- 2 tablespoons olive oil
- ½ teaspoon salt

- 1 teaspoon black pepper
- 2 garlic cloves, sliced
- 1 lemon, sliced, plus additional wedges for serving

Directions:

1. Preheat the air fryer to 190ºC.
2. Brush each fillet with olive oil on both sides and season with salt and pepper. Place the fillets in an even layer in the two air fryer baskets.
3. Place the sliced garlic over the tops of the trout fillets, then top the garlic with lemon slices and roast for 12 to 15 minutes, or until it has reached an internal temperature of 65ºC.
4. Serve with fresh lemon wedges.

Blackened Mahimahi With Honey-roasted Carrots

Servings:4
Cooking Time: 30 Minutes
Ingredients:

- FOR THE MAHIMAHI
- 4 mahimahi fillets (4 ounces each)
- 1 tablespoon olive oil
- 1 tablespoon blackening seasoning
- Lemon wedges, for serving
- FOR THE CARROTS
- 1 pound carrots, peeled and cut into ½-inch rounds

- 2 teaspoons vegetable oil
- ½ teaspoon kosher salt
- ¼ teaspoon freshly ground black pepper
- 1 tablespoon salted butter, cut into small pieces
- 1 tablespoon honey
- 2 tablespoons chopped fresh parsley

Directions:

1. To prep the mahimahi: Brush both sides of the fish with the oil and sprinkle with the blackening seasoning.
2. To prep the carrots: In a large bowl, combine the carrots, oil, salt, and black pepper. Stir well to coat the carrots with the oil.
3. To cook the mahimahi and carrots: Install a crisper plate in each of the two baskets. Place the fish in the Zone 1 basket and insert the basket in the unit. Place the carrots in the Zone 2 basket and insert the basket in the unit.
4. Select Zone 1, select AIR FRY, set the temperature to 380°F, and set the timer to 14 minutes.
5. Select Zone 2, select ROAST, set the temperature to 400°F, and set the timer to 30 minutes. Select SMART FINISH.
6. Press START/PAUSE to begin cooking.
7. When the Zone 2 timer reads 15 minutes, press START/PAUSE. Remove the basket and scatter the butter over the carrots, then drizzle them with the honey. Reinsert the basket and press START/PAUSE to resume cooking.
8. When cooking is complete, the fish should be cooked through and the carrots soft.
9. Stir the parsley into the carrots. Serve the fish with lemon wedges.

Nutrition:

- (Per serving) Calories: 235; Total fat: 9.5g; Saturated fat: 3g; Carbohydrates: 15g; Fiber: 3g; Protein: 22g; Sodium: 672mg

Salmon Fritters With Courgette & Cajun And Lemon Pepper Cod

Servings: 6

Cooking Time: 12 Minutes

Ingredients:

- Salmon Fritters with Courgette:
- 2 tablespoons almond flour
- 1 courgette, grated
- 1 egg, beaten
- 170 g salmon fillet, diced
- 1 teaspoon avocado oil
- ½ teaspoon ground black pepper
- Cajun and Lemon Pepper Cod:
- 1 tablespoon Cajun seasoning
- 1 teaspoon salt
- ½ teaspoon lemon pepper
- ½ teaspoon freshly ground black pepper
- 2 cod fillets, 230 g each, cut to fit into the air fryer basket
- Cooking spray
- 2 tablespoons unsalted butter, melted
- 1 lemon, cut into 4 wedges

Directions:

1. Make the Salmon Fritters with Courgette :
2. Mix almond flour with courgette, egg, salmon, and ground black pepper.
3. Then make the fritters from the salmon mixture.
4. Sprinkle the zone 1 air fryer basket with avocado oil and put the fritters inside.
5. Cook the fritters at 190°C for 6 minutes per side.
6. Make the Cajun and Lemon Pepper Cod :
7. Preheat the air fryer to 180°C. Spritz the zone 2 air fryer basket with cooking spray.
8. Thoroughly combine the Cajun seasoning, salt, lemon pepper, and black pepper in a small bowl. Rub this mixture all over the cod fillets until completely coated.
9. Put the fillets in the air fryer basket and brush the melted butter over both sides of each fillet.
10. Bake in the preheated air fryer for 12 minutes, flipping the fillets halfway through, or until the fish flakes easily with a fork.
11. Remove the fillets from the basket and serve with fresh lemon wedges.

Buttered Mahi-mahi

Servings: 4
Cooking Time: 22 Minutes
Ingredients:

- 4 (6-oz) mahi-mahi fillets
- Salt and black pepper ground to taste
- Cooking spray
- ⅔ cup butter

Directions:

1. Preheat your Ninja Foodi Dual Zone Air Fryer to 350 degrees F.
2. Rub the mahi-mahi fillets with salt and black pepper.
3. Place two mahi-mahi fillets in each of the crisper plate.
4. Return the crisper plates to the Ninja Foodi Dual Zone Air Fryer.
5. Choose the Air Fry mode for Zone 1 and set the temperature to 390 degrees F and the time to 17 minutes|
6. Select the "MATCH" button to copy the settings for Zone 2.
7. Initiate cooking by pressing the START/STOP button.
8. Add butter to a saucepan and cook for 5 minutes until slightly brown.
9. Remove the butter from the heat.
10. Drizzle butter over the fish and serve warm.

Salmon Nuggets

Servings: 4
Cooking Time: 15 Minutes
Ingredients:

- ⅓ cup maple syrup
- ¼ teaspoon dried chipotle pepper
- 1 pinch sea salt
- 1 ½ cups croutons
- 1 large egg
- 1 (1 pound) skinless salmon fillet, cut into 1 ½-inch chunk
- cooking spray

Directions:

1. Mix chipotle powder, maple syrup, and salt in a saucepan and cook on a simmer for 5 minutes|
2. Crush the croutons in a food processor and transfer to a bowl.
3. Beat egg in another shallow bowl.
4. Season the salmon chunks with sea salt.
5. Dip the salmon in the egg, then coat with breadcrumbs.
6. Divide the coated salmon chunks in the two crisper plates.
7. Return the crisper plate to the Ninja Foodi Dual Zone Air Fryer.
8. Select the Air Fry mode for Zone 1 and set the temperature to 390 degrees F and the time to 10 minutes|
9. Press the "MATCH" button to copy the settings for Zone 2.
10. Initiate cooking by pressing the START/STOP button.
11. Flip the chunks once cooked halfway through, then resume cooking.
12. Pour the maple syrup on top and serve warm.

Spicy Salmon Fillets

Servings: 6
Cooking Time: 8 Minutes
Ingredients:

- 900g salmon fillets
- ¾ tsp ground cumin
- 1 tbsp brown sugar
- 2 tbsp steak seasoning
- ¼ tsp cayenne pepper
- ½ tsp ground coriander

Directions:

1. Mix ground cumin, coriander, steak seasoning, brown sugar, and cayenne in a small bowl.
2. Rub salmon fillets with spice mixture.
3. Insert a crisper plate in the Ninja Foodi air fryer baskets.
4. Place the salmon fillets in both baskets.
5. Select zone 1, then select "bake" mode and set the temperature to 360 degrees F for 10 minutes. Press "match" to match zone 2 settings to zone 1. Press "start/stop" to begin.

Nutrition:

- (Per serving) Calories 207 | Fat 9.4g |Sodium 68mg | Carbs 1.6g | Fiber 0.1g | Sugar 1.5g | Protein 29.4g

Crispy Catfish

Servings: 4
Cooking Time: 17 Minutes
Ingredients:

- 4 catfish fillets
- ¼ cup Louisiana Fish fry
- 1 tablespoon olive oil
- 1 tablespoon parsley, chopped
- 1 lemon, sliced
- Fresh herbs, to garnish

Directions:

1. Mix fish fry with olive oil, and parsley then liberally rub over the catfish.
2. Place two fillets in each of the crisper plate.
3. Return the crisper plates to the Ninja Foodi Dual Zone Air Fryer.
4. Choose the Air Fry mode for Zone 1 and set the temperature to 390 degrees F and the time to 17 minutes|
5. Select the "MATCH" button to copy the settings for Zone 2.
6. Initiate cooking by pressing the START/STOP button.
7. Garnish with lemon slices and herbs.
8. Serve warm.

Parmesan Mackerel With Coriander And Garlic Butter Prawns Scampi

Servings: 6
Cooking Time: 8 Minutes

Ingredients:

- Parmesan Mackerel with Coriander:
- 340 g mackerel fillet
- 60 g Parmesan, grated
- 1 teaspoon ground coriander
- 1 tablespoon olive oil
- Garlic Butter Prawns Scampi:
- Sauce:
- 60 g unsalted butter
- 2 tablespoons fish stock or chicken broth
- 2 cloves garlic, minced
- 2 tablespoons chopped fresh basil leaves
- 1 tablespoon lemon juice
- 1 tablespoon chopped fresh parsley, plus more for garnish
- 1 teaspoon red pepper flakes
- Prawns:
- 455 g large prawns, peeled and deveined, tails removed
- Fresh basil sprigs, for garnish

Directions:

1. Make the Parmesan Mackerel with Coriander :
2. Sprinkle the mackerel fillet with olive oil and put it in the zone 1 air fryer drawer.
3. Top the fish with ground coriander and Parmesan.
4. Cook the fish at 200ºC for 7 minutes.
5. Make the Garlic Butter Prawns Scampi :
6. Preheat the zone 2 air fryer drawer to 176ºC.
7. Put all the ingredients for the sauce in a baking pan and stir to incorporate.
8. Transfer the baking pan to the zone 2 air fryer drawer and air fry for 3 minutes, or until the sauce is heated through.
9. Once done, add the prawns to the baking pan, flipping to coat in the sauce.
10. Return to the air fryer and cook for another 5 minutes, or until the prawns are pink and opaque. Stir the prawns twice during cooking.
11. Serve garnished with the parsley and basil sprigs.

Perfect Parmesan Salmon

Servings: 4
Cooking Time:10 Minutes
Ingredients:
- 4 salmon fillets
- 1/4 cup parmesan cheese, shredded
- 1/4 tsp dried dill
- 1/2 tbsp Dijon mustard
- 4 tbsp mayonnaise
- 1 lemon juice
- Pepper
- Salt

Directions:
1. In a small bowl, mix cheese, dill, mustard, mayonnaise, lemon juice, pepper, and salt.
2. Place salmon fillets into the air fryer basket and brush with cheese mixture.
3. Cook salmon fillets at 400 F for 10 minutes.
4. Serve and enjoy.

Glazed Scallops

Servings: 6
Cooking Time: 13 Minutes
Ingredients:
- 12 scallops
- 3 tablespoons olive oil
- Black pepper and salt to taste

Directions:
1. Rub the scallops with olive oil, black pepper, and salt.
2. Divide the scallops in the two crisper plates.
3. Return the crisper plate to the Ninja Foodi Dual Zone Air Fryer.
4. Choose the Air Fry mode for Zone 1 and set the temperature to 390 degrees F and the time to 13 minutes|
5. Select the "MATCH" button to copy the settings for Zone 2.
6. Initiate cooking by pressing the START/STOP button.
7. Flip the scallops once cooked halfway through, and resume cooking.
8. Serve warm.

Scallops And Spinach With Cream Sauce And Confetti Salmon Burgers

Servings: 6

Cooking Time: 12 Minutes

Ingredients:

- Scallops and Spinach with Cream Sauce:
- Vegetable oil spray
- 280 g frozen spinach, thawed and drained
- 8 jumbo sea scallops
- Kosher or coarse sea salt, and black pepper, to taste
- 180 ml heavy cream
- 1 tablespoon tomato paste
- 1 tablespoon chopped fresh basil
- 1 teaspoon minced garlic
- Confetti Salmon Burgers:
- 400 g cooked fresh or canned salmon, flaked with a fork
- 40 g minced spring onions, white and light green parts only
- 40 g minced red bell pepper
- 40 g minced celery
- 2 small lemons
- 1 teaspoon crab boil seasoning such as Old Bay
- ½ teaspoon kosher or coarse sea salt
- ½ teaspoon black pepper
- 1 egg, beaten
- 30 g fresh bread crumbs
- Vegetable oil, for spraying

Directions:

1. Make the Scallops and Spinach with Cream Sauce :
2. Spray a baking pan with vegetable oil spray. Spread the thawed spinach in an even layer in the bottom of the pan.
3. Spray both sides of the scallops with vegetable oil spray. Season lightly with salt and pepper. Arrange the scallops on top of the spinach.
4. In a small bowl, whisk together the cream, tomato paste, basil, garlic, ½ teaspoon salt, and ½ teaspoon pepper. Pour the sauce over the scallops and spinach.
5. Place the pan in the zone 1 air fryer drawer. Set the temperature to 176ºC for 10 minutes. Use a meat thermometer to ensure the scallops have an internal temperature of 56ºC.
6. Make the Confetti Salmon Burgers :
7. In a large bowl, combine the salmon, vegetables, the zest and juice of 1 of the lemons, crab boil seasoning, salt, and pepper. Add the egg and bread crumbs and stir to combine. Form the mixture into 4 patties weighing approximately 140 g each. Chill until firm, about 15 minutes.
8. Preheat the 2 air fryer drawer to 204ºC.
9. Spray the salmon patties with oil on all sides and spray the zone 2 air fryer drawer to prevent sticking. Air fry for 12 minutes, flipping halfway through, until the burgers are browned and cooked through. Cut the remaining lemon into 4 wedges and serve with the burgers.

Beer Battered Fish Fillet

Servings:2
Cooking Time:14

Ingredients:

- 1 cup all-purpose flour
- 4 tablespoons cornstarch
- 1 teaspoon baking soda
- 8 ounces beer
- 2 egg beaten
- ½ cup all-purpose flour
- 1 teaspoon smoked paprika
- 1 teaspoon salt
- 1/4 teaspoon freshly ground black pepper
- ¼ teaspoon of cayenne pepper
- 2 cod fillets, 1½-inches thick, cut into 4 pieces
- Oil spray, for greasing

Directions:

1. Take a large bowl and combine flour, baking soda, corn starch, and salt
2. In a separate bowl beat eggs along with the beer.
3. In a shallow dish mix paprika, salt, pepper, and cayenne pepper.
4. Dry the codfish fillets with a paper towel.
5. Dip the fish into the eggs and coat it with seasoned flour.
6. Then dip it in the seasoning.
7. Grease the fillet with oil spray.
8. Divide the fillet between both zones.
9. Set zone 1 to AIR FRY mode at 400 degrees F for 14 minutes.
10. Select MACTH button for zone 2 basket.
11. Press start and let the AIR fry do its magic.
12. Once cooking is done, serve the fish.
13. Enjoy it hot.

Nutrition:

- (Per serving) Calories 1691| Fat 6.1g| Sodium 3976mg | Carbs105.1 g | Fiber 3.4g | Sugar15.6 g | Protein 270g

Crispy Fish Nuggets

Servings: 4
Cooking Time: 8 Minutes
Ingredients:

- 2 eggs
- 96g all-purpose flour
- 700g cod fish fillets, cut into pieces
- 1 tsp garlic powder
- 1 tbsp old bay seasoning
- Pepper
- Salt

Directions:

1. In a small bowl, whisk eggs.
2. Mix flour, garlic powder, old bay seasoning, pepper, and salt in a shallow dish.
3. Coat each fish piece with flour, then dip in egg and again coat with flour.
4. Insert a crisper plate in the Ninja Foodi air fryer baskets.
5. Place coated fish pieces in both baskets.
6. Select zone 1, then select "air fry" mode and set the temperature to 380 degrees F for 8 minutes. Press "match" to match zone 2 settings to zone 1. Press "start/stop" to begin.

Nutrition:

- (Per serving) Calories 298 | Fat 3.9g |Sodium 683mg | Carbs 18.6g | Fiber 0.7g | Sugar 0.4g | Protein 44.1g

Pretzel-crusted Catfish

Servings: 4
Cooking Time: 12 Minutes
Ingredients:

- 4 catfish fillets
- ½ teaspoon salt
- ½ teaspoon black pepper
- 2 large eggs
- ⅓ cup Dijon mustard
- 2 tablespoons 2% milk
- ½ cup all-purpose flour
- 4 cups miniature pretzels, crushed
- Cooking spray
- Lemon slices

Directions:

1. Rub the catfish with black pepper and salt.
2. Beat eggs with milk and mustard in a bowl.
3. Spread pretzels and flour in two separate bowls.
4. Coat the catfish with flour then dip in the egg mixture and coat with the pretzels.
5. Place two fish fillets in each air fryer basket.
6. Return the air fryer basket 1 to Zone 1, and basket 2 to Zone 2 of the Ninja Foodi 2-Basket Air Fryer.
7. Choose the "Air Fry" mode for Zone 1 at 325 degrees F and 12 minutes of cooking time.
8. Select the "MATCH COOK" option to copy the settings for Zone 2.
9. Initiate cooking by pressing the START/PAUSE BUTTON.
10. Serve warm.

Nutrition:

- (Per serving) Calories 196 | Fat 7.1g |Sodium 492mg | Carbs 21.6g | Fiber 2.9g | Sugar 0.8g | Protein 13.4g

Panko-crusted Fish Sticks

Servings: 4
Cooking Time: 15 Minutes
Ingredients:

- Tartar Sauce:
- 470 ml mayonnaise
- 2 tablespoons dill pickle relish
- 1 tablespoon dried minced onions
- Fish Sticks:
- Olive or vegetable oil, for spraying
- 455 g tilapia fillets
- 75 g plain flour
- 120 g panko bread crumbs
- 2 tablespoons Creole seasoning
- 2 teaspoons garlic granules
- 1 teaspoon onion powder
- ½ teaspoon salt
- ¼ teaspoon freshly ground black pepper
- 1 large egg

Directions:

1. Make the Tartar Sauce: In a small bowl, whisk together the mayonnaise, pickle relish, and onions. Cover with plastic wrap and refrigerate until ready to serve. You can make this sauce ahead of time; the flavors will intensify as it chills. Make the Fish Sticks: 2. Preheat the air fryer to 175ºC. Line the two air fryer baskets with baking paper and spray lightly with oil. 3. Cut the fillets into equal-size sticks and place them in a zip-top plastic bag. 4. Add the flour to the bag, seal, and shake well until evenly coated. 5. In a shallow bowl, mix together the bread crumbs, Creole seasoning, garlic, onion powder, salt, and black pepper. 6. In a small bowl, whisk the egg. 7. Dip the fish sticks in the egg, then dredge in the bread crumb mixture until completely coated. 8. Place the fish sticks in the two prepared baskets. Do not overcrowd. Spray lightly with oil. 9. Cook for 12 to 15 minutes, or until browned and cooked through. Serve with the tartar sauce.

Orange-mustard Glazed Salmon And Cucumber And Salmon Salad

Servings: 4

Cooking Time: 10 Minutes

Ingredients:

- Orange-Mustard Glazed Salmon:
- 1 tablespoon orange marmalade
- ¼ teaspoon grated orange zest plus 1 tablespoon juice
- 2 teaspoons whole-grain mustard
- 2 (230 g) skin-on salmon fillets, 1½ inches thick
- Salt and pepper, to taste
- Vegetable oil spray
- Cucumber and Salmon Salad:
- 455 g salmon fillet
- 1½ tablespoons olive oil, divided
- 1 tablespoon sherry vinegar
- 1 tablespoon capers, rinsed and drained
- 1 seedless cucumber, thinly sliced
- ¼ white onion, thinly sliced
- 2 tablespoons chopped fresh parsley
- Salt and freshly ground black pepper, to taste

Directions:

1. Make the Orange-Mustard Glazed Salmon :
2. Preheat the air fryer to 205ºC.
3. Make foil sling for air fryer basket by folding 1 long sheet of aluminum foil so it is 4 inches wide. Lay sheet of foil widthwise across zone 1 basket, pressing foil into and up sides of basket. Fold excess foil as needed so that edges of foil are flush with top of basket. Lightly spray foil and basket with vegetable oil spray.
4. Combine marmalade, orange zest and juice, and mustard in bowl. Pat salmon dry with paper towels and season with salt and pepper. Brush tops and sides of fillets evenly with glaze. Arrange fillets skin side down on sling in prepared zone 1 basket, spaced evenly apart. Air fry salmon until center is still translucent when checked with the tip of a paring knife and registers 50ºC , 10 to 14 minutes, using sling to rotate fillets halfway through cooking.
5. Using the sling, carefully remove salmon from air fryer. Slide fish spatula along underside of fillets and transfer to individual serving plates, leaving skin behind. Serve.
6. Make the Cucumber and Salmon Salad :
7. Preheat the air fryer to 205ºC.
8. Lightly coat the salmon with ½ tablespoon of the olive oil. Place skin-side down in the zone 2 air fryer basket and air fry for 8 to 10 minutes until the fish is opaque and flakes easily with a fork. Transfer the salmon to a plate and let cool to room temperature. Remove the skin and carefully flake the fish into bite-size chunks.
9. In a small bowl, whisk the remaining 1 tablespoon olive oil and the vinegar until thoroughly combined. Add the flaked fish, capers, cucumber, onion, and parsley. Season to taste with salt and freshly ground black pepper. Toss gently to coat. Serve immediately or cover and refrigerate for up to 4 hours.

Vegetables And Sides Recipes
Green Beans With Baked Potatoes

Servings: 2
Cooking Time: 45 Minutes
Ingredients:

- 2 cups green beans
- 2 large potatoes, cubed
- 3 tablespoons olive oil
- 1 teaspoon seasoned salt
- ½ teaspoon chili powder
- ⅛ teaspoon garlic powder
- ¼ teaspoon onion powder

Directions:

1. Take a large bowl and pour olive oil into it.
2. Add all the seasoning in the olive oil and whisk it well.
3. Toss the green beans in and mix well and then transfer to zone 1 basket of the air fryer.
4. Season the potatoes with the oil seasoning and add them to the zone 2 basket.
5. Press the Sync button.
6. Once the cooking cycle is complete, take out and serve.

Lime Glazed Tofu

Servings: 6
Cooking Time: 14 Minutes
Ingredients:

- ⅔ cup coconut aminos
- 2 (14-oz) packages extra-firm, water-packed tofu, drained
- 6 tablespoons toasted sesame oil
- ⅔ cup lime juice

Directions:

1. Pat dry the tofu bars and slice into half-inch cubes.
2. Toss all the remaining ingredients in a small bowl.
3. Marinate for 4 hours in the refrigerator. Drain off the excess water.
4. Divide the tofu cubes in the two crisper plates.
5. Return the crisper plates to the Ninja Foodi Dual Zone Air Fryer.
6. Choose the Air Fry mode for Zone 1 and set the temperature to 400 degrees F/ 200 degrees C and the time to 14 minutes.
7. Select the "MATCH" button to copy the settings for Zone 2.
8. Initiate cooking by pressing the START/STOP button.
9. Toss the tofu once cooked halfway through, then resume cooking. 10. Serve warm.

Broccoli, Squash, & Pepper

Servings: 4
Cooking Time: 12 Minutes
Ingredients:

- 175g broccoli florets
- 1 red bell pepper, diced
- 1 tbsp olive oil
- ½ tsp garlic powder
- ¼ onion, sliced

- 1 zucchini, sliced
- 2 yellow squash, sliced
- Pepper
- Salt

Directions:

1. In a bowl, toss veggies with oil, garlic powder, pepper, and salt.
2. Insert a crisper plate in the Ninja Foodi air fryer baskets.
3. Add the vegetable mixture in both baskets.
4. Select zone 1 then select "air fry" mode and set the temperature to 390 degrees F for 12 minutes. Press "match" to match zone 2 settings to zone 1. Press "start/stop" to begin. Stir halfway through.

Nutrition:

- (Per serving) Calories 75 | Fat 3.9g |Sodium 62mg | Carbs 9.6g | Fiber 2.8g | Sugar 4.8g | Protein 2.9g

Fried Olives

Servings: 6
Cooking Time: 9 Minutes
Ingredients:

- 2 cups blue cheese stuffed olives, drained
- ½ cup all-purpose flour
- 1 cup panko breadcrumbs
- ½ teaspoon garlic powder
- 1 pinch oregano
- 2 eggs

Directions:

1. Mix flour with oregano and garlic powder in a bowl and beat two eggs in another bowl.
2. Spread panko breadcrumbs in a bowl.
3. Coat all the olives with the flour mixture, dip in the eggs and then coat with the panko breadcrumbs.
4. As you coat the olives, place them in the two crisper plates in a single layer, then spray them with cooking oil.
5. Return the crisper plates to the Ninja Foodi Dual Zone Air Fryer.
6. Choose the Air Fry mode for Zone 1 and set the temperature to 375 degrees F/ 190 degrees C and the time to 9 minutes.
7. Select the "MATCH" button to copy the settings for Zone 2.
8. Initiate cooking by pressing the START/STOP button.
9. Flip the olives once cooked halfway through, then resume cooking.
10. Serve.

Lemon Herb Cauliflower

Servings: 4
Cooking Time: 10 Minutes

Ingredients:

- 384g cauliflower florets
- 1 tsp lemon zest, grated
- 1 tbsp thyme, minced
- 60ml olive oil
- 1 tbsp rosemary, minced
- ¼ tsp red pepper flakes, crushed
- 30ml lemon juice
- 25g parsley, minced
- ½ tsp salt

Directions:

1. In a bowl, toss cauliflower florets with the remaining ingredients until well coated.
2. Insert a crisper plate in the Ninja Foodi air fryer baskets.
3. Add cauliflower florets into both baskets.
4. Select zone 1, then select "air fry" mode and set the temperature to 360 degrees F for 10 minutes. Press "match" and "start/stop" to begin.

Nutrition:

- (Per serving) Calories 166 | Fat 14.4g |Sodium 340mg | Carbs 9.5g | Fiber 4.6g | Sugar 3.8g | Protein 3.3g

Balsamic Vegetables

Servings: 4
Cooking Time: 13 Minutes

Ingredients:

- 125g asparagus, cut woody ends
- 88g mushrooms, halved
- 1 tbsp Dijon mustard
- 3 tbsp soy sauce
- 27g brown sugar
- 57ml balsamic vinegar
- 32g olive oil
- 1 zucchini, sliced
- 1 yellow squash, sliced
- 170g grape tomatoes
- Pepper
- Salt

Directions:

1. In a bowl, mix asparagus, tomatoes, oil, mustard, soy sauce, mushrooms, zucchini, squash, brown sugar, vinegar, pepper, and salt.
2. Cover the bowl and place it in the refrigerator for 45 minutes.
3. Insert a crisper plate in the Ninja Foodi air fryer baskets.
4. Add the vegetable mixture in both baskets.
5. Select zone 1, then select "air fry" mode and set the temperature to 390 degrees F for 12 minutes. Press "match" to match zone 2 settings to zone 1. Press "start/stop" to begin. Stir halfway through.

Nutrition:

- (Per serving) Calories 184 | Fat 13.3g |Sodium 778mg | Carbs 14.7g | Fiber 3.6g | Sugar 9.5g | Protein 5.5g

Beets With Orange Gremolata And Goat's Cheese

Servings: 12
Cooking Time: 45 Minutes
Ingredients:

- 3 medium fresh golden beets (about 1 pound)
- 3 medium fresh beets (about 1 pound)
- 2 tablespoons lime juice
- 2 tablespoons orange juice
- ½ teaspoon fine sea salt
- 1 tablespoon minced fresh parsley
- 1 tablespoon minced fresh sage
- 1 garlic clove, minced
- 1 teaspoon grated orange zest
- 3 tablespoons crumbled goat's cheese
- 2 tablespoons sunflower kernels

Directions:

1. Scrub the beets and trim the tops by 1 inch.
2. Place the beets on a double thickness of heavy-duty foil . Fold the foil around the beets, sealing tightly.
3. Place a crisper plate in both drawers. Put the beets in a single layer in each drawer. Insert the drawers into the unit.
4. Select zone 1, then AIR FRY, then set the temperature to 360 degrees F/ 180 degrees C with a 45-minute timer. To match zone 2 settings to zone 1, choose MATCH. To begin, select START/STOP.
5. Remove the beets from the drawers after the timer has finished. Peel, halve, and slice them when they're cool enough to handle. Place them in a serving bowl.
6. Toss in the lime juice, orange juice, and salt to coat. Sprinkle the beets with the parsley, sage, garlic, and orange zest. The sunflower kernels and goat's cheese go on top.

Garlic Herbed Baked Potatoes

Servings: 4
Cooking Time: 45 Minutes
Ingredients:

- 4 large baking potatoes
- Salt and black pepper, to taste
- 2 teaspoons avocado oil
- Cheese
- 2 cups sour cream
- 1 teaspoon garlic clove, minced
- 1 teaspoon fresh dill
- 2 teaspoons chopped chives
- Salt and black pepper, to taste
- 2 teaspoons Worcestershire sauce

Directions:

1. Pierce the skin of the potatoes with a fork.
2. Season the potatoes with olive oil, salt, and black pepper.
3. Divide the potatoes into the air fryer baskets.
4. Now press 1 for zone 1 and set it to AIR FRY mode at 350 degrees F/ 175 degrees C, for 45 minutes.
5. Select the MATCH button for zone 2.
6. Meanwhile, take a bowl and mix all the cheese ingredients together.
7. Once the cooking cycle is complete, take out the potatoes and make a slit in-between each one.
8. Add the cheese mixture in the cavity and serve it hot.

Fried Patty Pan Squash

Servings: 6

Cooking Time: 15 Minutes

Ingredients:

- 5 cups small pattypan squash, halved
- 1 tablespoon olive oil
- 2 garlic cloves, minced
- ½ teaspoon salt
- ¼ teaspoon dried oregano
- ¼ teaspoon dried thyme
- ¼ teaspoon pepper
- 1 tablespoon minced parsley

Directions:

1. Rub the squash with oil, garlic and the rest of the ingredients.
2. Spread the squash in the air fryer baskets.
3. Return the air fryer basket 1 to Zone 1, and basket 2 to Zone 2 of the Ninja Foodi 2-Basket Air Fryer.
4. Choose the "Air Fry" mode for Zone 1 at 375 degrees F and 15 minutes of cooking time.
5. Select the "MATCH COOK" option to copy the settings for Zone 2.
6. Initiate cooking by pressing the START/PAUSE BUTTON.
7. Flip the squash once cooked halfway through.
8. Garnish with parsley.
9. Serve warm.

Nutrition:

- (Per serving) Calories 208 | Fat 5g |Sodium 1205mg | Carbs 34.1g | Fiber 7.8g | Sugar 2.5g | Protein 5.9g

Air-fried Tofu Cutlets With Cacio E Pepe Brussels Sprouts

Servings:4

Cooking Time: 25 Minutes

Ingredients:

- FOR THE TOFU CUTLETS
- 1 (14-ounce) package extra-firm tofu, drained
- 1 cup panko bread crumbs
- ¼ cup grated pecorino romano or Parmesan cheese
- 1 teaspoon garlic powder
- 1 teaspoon onion powder
- ¼ teaspoon kosher salt
- 1 tablespoon vegetable oil
- 4 lemon wedges, for serving
- FOR THE BRUSSELS SPROUTS
- 1 pound Brussels sprouts, trimmed
- 1 tablespoon vegetable oil
- 2 tablespoons grated pecorino romano or Parmesan cheese
- ½ teaspoon freshly ground black pepper, plus more to taste
- ¼ teaspoon kosher salt

Directions:

1. To prep the tofu: Cut the tofu horizontally into 4 slabs.

2. In a shallow bowl, mix together the panko, cheese, garlic powder, onion powder, and salt. Press both sides of each tofu slab into the panko mixture. Drizzle both sides with the oil.

3. To prep the Brussels sprouts: Cut the Brussels sprouts in half through the root end.

4. In a large bowl, combine the Brussels sprouts and olive oil. Mix to coat.

5. To cook the tofu cutlets and Brussels sprouts: Install a crisper plate in each of the two baskets. Place the tofu cutlets in a single layer in the Zone 1 basket and insert the basket in the unit. Place the Brussels sprouts in the Zone 2 basket and insert the basket in the unit.

6. Select Zone 1, select AIR FRY, set the temperature to 400°F, and set the timer to 20 minutes.

7. Select Zone 2, select ROAST, set the temperature to 400°F, and set the timer to 25 minutes. Select SMART FINISH.

8. Press START/PAUSE to begin cooking.

9. When both timers read 5 minutes, press START/PAUSE. Remove the Zone 1 basket and use a pair of silicone-tipped tongs to flip the tofu cutlets, then reinsert the basket in the unit. Remove the Zone 2 basket and sprinkle the cheese and black pepper over the Brussels sprouts. Reinsert the basket and press START/PAUSE to resume cooking.

10. When cooking is complete, the tofu should be crisp and the Brussels sprouts tender and beginning to brown.

11. Squeeze the lemon wedges over the tofu cutlets. Stir the Brussels sprouts, then season with the salt and additional black pepper to taste.

Nutrition:

- (Per serving) Calories: 319; Total fat: 15g; Saturated fat: 3.5g; Carbohydrates: 27g; Fiber: 6g; Protein: 20g; Sodium: 402mg

Saucy Carrots

Servings: 6
Cooking Time: 25 Minutes
Ingredients:

- 1 lb. cup carrots, cut into chunks
- 1 tablespoon sesame oil
- ½ tablespoon ginger, minced
- ½ tablespoon soy sauce
- ½ teaspoon garlic, minced
- ½ tablespoon scallions, chopped, for garnish
- ½ teaspoon sesame seeds for garnish

Directions:

1. Toss all the ginger carrots ingredients, except the sesame seeds and scallions, in a suitable bowl.
2. Divide the carrots in the two crisper plates in a single layer.
3. Return the crisper plates to the Ninja Foodi Dual Zone Air Fryer.
4. Choose the Air Fry mode for Zone 1 and set the temperature to 390 degrees F/ 200 degrees C and the time to 25 minutes.
5. Select the "MATCH" button to copy the settings for Zone 2.
6. Initiate cooking by pressing the START/STOP button.
7. Toss the carrots once cooked halfway through.
8. Garnish with sesame seeds and scallions.
9. Serve warm.

Air Fried Okra

Servings: 2
Cooking Time: 13 Minutes
Ingredients:

- ½ lb. okra pods sliced
- 1 teaspoon olive oil
- ¼ teaspoon salt
- ⅛ teaspoon black pepper

Directions:

1. Preheat the Ninja Foodi Dual Zone Air Fryer to 350 degrees F/ 175 degrees C.
2. Toss okra with olive oil, salt, and black pepper in a bowl.
3. Spread the okra in a single layer in the two crisper plates.
4. Return the crisper plate to the Ninja Foodi Dual Zone Air Fryer.
5. Choose the Air Fry mode for Zone 1 and set the temperature to 375 degrees F/ 190 degrees C and the time to 13 minutes.
6. Select the "MATCH" button to copy the settings for Zone 2.
7. Initiate cooking by pressing the START/STOP button.
8. Toss the okra once cooked halfway through, and resume cooking.
9. Serve warm.

Buffalo Seitan With Crispy Zucchini Noodles

Servings:4

Cooking Time: 12 Minutes

Ingredients:

- FOR THE BUFFALO SEITAN
- 1 (8-ounce) package precooked seitan strips
- 1 teaspoon garlic powder, divided
- ½ teaspoon onion powder
- ¼ teaspoon smoked paprika
- ¼ cup Louisiana-style hot sauce
- 2 tablespoons vegetable oil
- 1 tablespoon tomato paste
- ¼ teaspoon freshly ground black pepper
- FOR THE ZUCCHINI NOODLES
- 3 large egg whites
- 1¼ cups all-purpose flour
- 1 teaspoon kosher salt, divided
- 12 ounces seltzer water or club soda
- 5 ounces zucchini noodles
- Nonstick cooking spray

Directions:

1. To prep the Buffalo seitan: Season the seitan strips with ½ teaspoon of garlic powder, the onion powder, and smoked paprika.

2. In a large bowl, whisk together the hot sauce, oil, tomato paste, remaining ½ teaspoon of garlic powder, and the black pepper. Set the bowl of Buffalo sauce aside.

3. To prep the zucchini noodles: In a medium bowl, use a handheld mixer to beat the egg whites until stiff peaks form.

4. In a large bowl, combine the flour and ½ teaspoon of salt. Mix in the seltzer to form a thin batter. Fold in the beaten egg whites.

5. Add the zucchini to the batter and gently mix to coat.

6. To cook the seitan and zucchini noodles: Install a crisper plate in each of the two baskets. Place the seitan in the Zone 1 basket and insert the basket in the unit. Lift the noodles from the batter one at a time, letting the excess drip off, and place them in the Zone 2 basket. Insert the basket in the unit.

7. Select Zone 1, select BAKE, set the temperature to 370°F, and set the timer to 12 minutes.

8. Select Zone 2, select AIR FRY, set the temperature to 400°F, and set the timer to 12 minutes. Select SMART FINISH.

9. Press START/PAUSE to begin cooking.

10. When the Zone 1 timer reads 2 minutes, press START/PAUSE. Remove the basket and transfer the seitan to the bowl of Buffalo sauce. Turn to coat, then return the seitan to the basket. Reinsert the basket and press START/PAUSE to resume cooking.

11. When cooking is complete, the seitan should be warmed through and the zucchini noodles crisp and light golden brown.

12. Sprinkle the zucchini noodles with the remaining ½ teaspoon of salt. If desired, drizzle extra Buffalo sauce over the seitan. Serve hot.

Nutrition:

- (Per serving) Calories: 252; Total fat: 15g; Saturated fat: 1g; Carbohydrates: 22g; Fiber: 1.5g; Protein: 13g; Sodium: 740mg

Rosemary Asparagus & Potatoes

Servings: 6
Cooking Time: 30 Minutes

Ingredients:

- 125g asparagus, trimmed & cut into pieces
- 2 tsp garlic powder
- 2 tbsp rosemary, chopped
- 30ml olive oil
- 679g baby potatoes, quartered
- ½ tsp red pepper flakes
- Pepper
- Salt

Directions:

1. Insert a crisper plate in the Ninja Foodi air fryer baskets.
2. Toss potatoes with 1 tablespoon of oil, pepper, and salt in a bowl until well coated.
3. Add potatoes into in zone 1 basket.
4. Toss asparagus with remaining oil, red pepper flakes, pepper, garlic powder, and rosemary in a mixing bowl.
5. Add asparagus into the zone 2 basket.
6. Select zone 1, then select "air fry" mode and set the temperature to 390 degrees F for 20 minutes. Select zone 2, then select "air fry" mode and set the temperature to 390 degrees F for 10 minutes. Press "match" mode, then press "start/stop" to begin.

Nutrition:

- (Per serving) Calories 121 | Fat 5g |Sodium 40mg | Carbs 17.1g | Fiber 4.2g | Sugar 1g | Protein 4g

Brussels Sprouts

Servings: 2
Cooking Time: 20 Minutes

Ingredients:

- 2 pounds Brussels sprouts
- 2 tablespoons avocado oil
- Salt and pepper, to taste
- 1 cup pine nuts, roasted

Directions:

1. Trim the bottom of the Brussels sprouts.
2. Take a bowl and combine the avocado oil, salt, and black pepper.
3. Toss the Brussels sprouts into the bowl and mix well.
4. Divide the mixture into both air fryer baskets.
5. For zone 1 set to AIR FRY mode for 20 minutes at 390 degrees F/ 200 degrees C.
6. Select the MATCH button for the zone 2 basket.
7. Once the Brussels sprouts get crisp and tender, take out and serve.

Spanakopita Rolls With Mediterranean Vegetable Salad

Servings:4

Cooking Time: 15 Minutes

Ingredients:

- FOR THE SPANAKOPITA ROLLS
- 1 (10-ounce) package chopped frozen spinach, thawed
- 4 ounces feta cheese, crumbled
- 2 large eggs
- 1 teaspoon dried oregano
- ½ teaspoon freshly ground black pepper
- 12 sheets phyllo dough, thawed
- 1 (15-ounce) can chickpeas, drained and rinsed
- ¼ cup chopped fresh parsley
- ¼ cup olive oil
- ¼ cup red wine vinegar
- 2 garlic cloves, minced
- ½ teaspoon dried oregano
- ¼ teaspoon kosher salt
- ¼ teaspoon freshly ground black pepper
- Nonstick cooking spray
- FOR THE ROASTED VEGETABLES
- 1 medium eggplant, diced
- 1 small red onion, cut into 8 wedges
- 1 red bell pepper, sliced
- 2 tablespoons olive oil
- FOR THE SALAD

Directions:

1. To prep the spanakopita rolls: Squeeze as much liquid from the spinach as you can and place the spinach in a large bowl. Add the feta, eggs, oregano, and black pepper. Mix well.

2. Lay one sheet of phyllo on a clean work surface and mist it with cooking spray. Place another sheet of phyllo directly on top of the first sheet and mist it with cooking spray. Repeat with a third sheet.

3. Spoon one-quarter of the spinach mixture along one short side of the phyllo. Fold the long sides in over the spinach, then roll up it like a burrito.

4. Repeat this process with the remaining phyllo sheets and spinach mixture to form 4 rolls.

5. To prep the vegetables: In a large bowl, combine the eggplant, onion, bell pepper, and oil. Mix well.

6. To cook the rolls and vegetables: Install a crisper plate in each of the two baskets. Place the spanakopita rolls seam-side down in the Zone 1 basket, and spritz the rolls with cooking spray. Place the vegetables in the Zone 2 basket and insert both baskets in the unit.

7. Select Zone 1, select AIR FRY, set the temperature to 375°F, and set the timer to 10 minutes.

8. Select Zone 2, select ROAST, set the temperature to 375°F, and set the timer to 15 minutes. Select SMART FINISH.

9. Press START/PAUSE to begin cooking.

10. When the Zone 1 timer reads 3 minutes, press START/PAUSE. Remove the basket and use silicone-tipped tongs or a spatula to flip the spanakopita rolls. Reinsert the basket and press START/PAUSE to resume cooking.

11. When cooking is complete, the rolls should be crisp and golden brown and the vegetables tender.

12. To assemble the salad: Transfer the roasted vegetables to a large bowl. Stir in the chickpeas and parsley.

13. In a small bowl, whisk together the oil, vinegar, garlic, oregano, salt, and black pepper. Pour the dressing over the vegetables and toss to coat. Serve warm.

Nutrition:

- (Per serving) Calories: 739; Total fat: 51g; Saturated fat: 8g; Carbohydrates: 67g; Fiber: 11g; Protein: 21g; Sodium: 806mg

Curly Fries

Servings: 6
Cooking Time: 20 Minutes
Ingredients:

- 2 spiralized zucchinis
- 1 cup flour
- 2 tablespoons paprika
- 1 teaspoon cayenne pepper
- 1 teaspoon garlic powder

- 1 teaspoon black pepper
- 1 teaspoon salt
- 2 eggs
- Olive oil or cooking spray

Directions:

1. Mix flour with paprika, cayenne pepper, garlic powder, black pepper, and salt in a bowl.
2. Beat eggs in another bowl and dip the zucchini in the eggs.
3. Coat the zucchini with the flour mixture and divide it into two crisper plates. 4. Spray the zucchini with cooking oil.
4. Return the crisper plate to the Ninja Foodi Dual Zone Air Fryer.
5. Choose the Air Fry mode for Zone 1 and set the temperature to 400 degrees F/ 200 degrees C and the time to 20 minutes.
6. Select the "MATCH" button to copy the settings for Zone 2.
7. Initiate cooking by pressing the START/STOP button.
8. Toss the zucchini once cooked halfway through, then resume cooking.
9. Serve warm.

Zucchini Cakes

Servings: 6
Cooking Time: 32 Minutes
Ingredients:

- 2 medium zucchinis, grated
- 1 cup corn kernel
- 1 medium potato cooked
- 2 tablespoons chickpea flour
- 2 garlic minced

- 2 teaspoons olive oil
- Salt and black pepper
- For Serving:
- Yogurt tahini sauce

Directions:

1. Mix grated zucchini with a pinch of salt in a colander and leave them for 15 minutes.
2. Squeeze out their excess water.
3. Mash the cooked potato in a large-sized bowl with a fork.
4. Add zucchini, corn, garlic, chickpea flour, salt, and black pepper to the bowl. 5. Mix these fritters' ingredients together and make 2 tablespoons-sized balls out of this mixture and flatten them lightly.
5. Divide the fritters in the two crisper plates in a single layer and spray them with cooking.
6. Return the crisper plates to the Ninja Foodi Dual Zone Air Fryer.
7. Choose the Air Fry mode for Zone 1 and set the temperature to 390 degrees F/ 200 degrees C and the time to 17 minutes.
8. Select the "MATCH" button to copy the settings for Zone 2.
9. Initiate cooking by pressing the START/STOP button.
10. Flip the fritters once cooked halfway through, then resume cooking.
11. Serve.

Acorn Squash Slices

Servings: 6
Cooking Time: 10 Minutes
Ingredients:

- 2 medium acorn squashes
- ⅔ cup packed brown sugar
- ½ cup butter, melted

Directions:

1. Cut the squash in half, remove the seeds and slice into ½ inch slices.
2. Place the squash slices in the air fryer baskets.
3. Drizzle brown sugar and butter over the squash slices.
4. Return the air fryer basket 1 to Zone 1, and basket 2 to Zone 2 of the Ninja Foodi 2-Basket Air Fryer.
5. Choose the "Air Fry" mode for Zone 1 and set the temperature to 350 degrees F and 10 minutes of cooking time.
6. Select the "MATCH COOK" option to copy the settings for Zone 2.
7. Initiate cooking by pressing the START/PAUSE BUTTON.
8. Flip the squash once cooked halfway through.
9. Serve.

Nutrition:

- (Per serving) Calories 206 | Fat 3.4g |Sodium 174mg | Carbs 35g | Fiber 9.4g | Sugar 5.9g | Protein 10.6g

Breaded Summer Squash

Servings: 4
Cooking Time: 10 Minutes
Ingredients:

- 4 cups yellow summer squash, sliced
- 3 tablespoons olive oil
- ½ teaspoon salt
- ½ teaspoon pepper
- ⅛ teaspoon cayenne pepper
- ¾ cup panko bread crumbs
- ¾ cup grated Parmesan cheese

Directions:

1. Mix crumbs, cheese, cayenne pepper, black pepper, salt and oil in a bowl.
2. Coat the squash slices with the breadcrumb mixture.
3. Place these slices in the air fryer baskets.
4. Return the air fryer basket 1 to Zone 1, and basket 2 to Zone 2 of the Ninja Foodi 2-Basket Air Fryer.
5. Choose the "Air Fry" mode for Zone 1 at 350 degrees F and 10 minutes of cooking time.
6. Select the "MATCH COOK" option to copy the settings for Zone 2.
7. Initiate cooking by pressing the START/PAUSE BUTTON.
8. Flip the squash slices once cooked half way through.
9. Serve warm.

Nutrition:

- (Per serving) Calories 193 | Fat 1g |Sodium 395mg | Carbs 38.7g | Fiber 1.6g | Sugar 0.9g | Protein 6.6g

Balsamic-glazed Tofu With Roasted Butternut Squash

Servings:4

Cooking Time: 40 Minutes

Ingredients:

- FOR THE BALSAMIC TOFU
- 2 tablespoons balsamic vinegar
- 1 tablespoon maple syrup
- 1 teaspoon soy sauce
- 1 teaspoon Dijon mustard
- 1 (14-ounce) package firm tofu, drained and cut into large cubes
- 1 tablespoon canola oil
- FOR THE BUTTERNUT SQUASH
- 1 small butternut squash
- 1 tablespoon canola oil
- 1 teaspoon light brown sugar
- ¼ teaspoon kosher salt
- ¼ teaspoon freshly ground black pepper

Directions:

1. To prep the balsamic tofu: In a large bowl, whisk together the vinegar, maple syrup, soy sauce, and mustard. Add the tofu and stir to coat. Cover and marinate for at least 20 minutes (or up to overnight in the refrigerator).

2. To prep the butternut squash: Peel the squash and cut in half lengthwise. Remove and discard the seeds. Cut the squash crosswise into ½-inch-thick slices.

3. Brush the squash pieces with the oil, then sprinkle with the brown sugar, salt, and black pepper.

4. To cook the tofu and squash: Install a crisper plate in each of the two baskets. Place the tofu in the Zone 1 basket, drizzle with the oil, and insert the basket in the unit. Place the squash in the Zone 2 basket and insert the basket in the unit.

5. Select Zone 1, select AIR FRY, set the temperature to 400°F, and set the timer to 10 minutes.

6. Select Zone 2, select ROAST, set the temperature to 400°F, and set the timer to 40 minutes. Select SMART FINISH.

7. Press START/PAUSE to begin cooking.

8. When cooking is complete, the tofu will have begun to crisp and brown around the edges and the squash should be tender. Serve hot.

Nutrition:

- (Per serving) Calories: 253; Total fat: 11g; Saturated fat: 1g; Carbohydrates: 30g; Fiber: 4.5g; Protein: 11g; Sodium: 237mg

Desserts Recipes
<u>Apple Fritters</u>

Servings: 14
Cooking Time: 10 Minutes
Ingredients:

- 2 large apples
- 2 cups all-purpose flour
- ½ cup granulated sugar
- 1 tablespoon baking powder
- 1 teaspoon salt
- 1 teaspoon ground cinnamon
- ½ teaspoon ground nutmeg
- ¼ teaspoon ground cloves
- ¾ cup apple cider or apple juice
- 2 eggs
- 3 tablespoons butter, melted
- 1 teaspoon vanilla extract
- For the apple cider glaze:
- 2 cups powdered sugar
- ¼ cup apple cider or apple juice
- ½ teaspoon ground cinnamon
- ¼ teaspoon ground nutmeg

Directions:

1. Peel and core the apples, then cut them into ¼-inch cubes. Spread the apple chunks out on a kitchen towel to absorb any excess moisture.
2. In a mixing bowl, combine the flour, sugar, baking powder, salt, and spices.
3. Add the apple chunks and combine well.
4. Whisk together the apple cider, eggs, melted butter, and vanilla in a small bowl.
5. Combine the wet and dry in a large mixing bowl.
6. Install a crisper plate in both drawers. Use an ice cream scoop to scoop 3 to 4 dollops of fritter dough into the zone 1 drawer and 3 to 4 dollops into the zone 2 drawer. Insert the drawers into the unit. You may need to cook in batches.
7. Select zone 1, select BAKE, set temperature to 390°F, and set time to 10 minutes. Select MATCH to match zone 2 settings to zone 1. Press the START/STOP button to begin cooking.
8. Meanwhile, make the glaze: Whisk the powdered sugar, apple cider, and spices together until smooth.
9. When the fritters are cooked, drizzle the glaze over them. Let sit for 10 minutes until the glaze sets.

Homemade Mint Pie And Strawberry Pecan Pie

Servings: 8

Cooking Time: 25 Minutes

Ingredients:

- Homemade Mint Pie:
- 1 tablespoon instant coffee
- 2 tablespoons almond butter, softened
- 2 tablespoons granulated sweetener
- 1 teaspoon dried mint
- 3 eggs, beaten
- 1 teaspoon dried spearmint
- 4 teaspoons coconut flour
- Cooking spray
- Strawberry Pecan Pie:
- 190 g whole shelled pecans
- 1 tablespoon unsalted butter, softened
- 240 ml heavy whipping cream
- 12 medium fresh strawberries, hulled
- 2 tablespoons sour cream

Directions:

1. Make the Homemade Mint Pie:
2. Spray the zone 1 air fryer drawer with cooking spray.
3. Then mix all ingredients in the mixer bowl.
4. When you get a smooth mixture, transfer it in the zone 1 air fryer drawer. Flatten it gently. Cook the pie at 185ºC for 25 minutes.
5. Make the Strawberry Pecan Pie:
6. Place pecans and butter into a food processor and pulse ten times until a dough forms. Press dough into the bottom of an ungreased round nonstick baking dish.
7. Place dish into the zone 2 air fryer drawer. Adjust the temperature to 160ºC and set the timer for 10 minutes. Crust will be firm and golden when done. Let cool 20 minutes.
8. In a large bowl, whisk cream until fluffy and doubled in size, about 2 minutes.
9. In a separate large bowl, mash strawberries until mostly liquid. Fold strawberries and sour cream into whipped cream.
10. Spoon mixture into cooled crust, cover, and place in refrigerator for at least 30 minutes to set. Serve chilled.

Cinnamon-sugar "churros" With Caramel Sauce

Servings:4

Cooking Time: 10 Minutes

Ingredients:

- FOR THE "CHURROS"
- 1 sheet frozen puff pastry, thawed
- Butter-flavored cooking spray
- 1 tablespoon granulated sugar
- 1 teaspoon ground cinnamon
- FOR THE CARAMEL SAUCE
- ½ cup packed light brown sugar
- 2 tablespoons unsalted butter, cut into small pieces
- ¼ cup heavy (whipping) cream
- 2 teaspoons vanilla extract
- ⅛ teaspoon kosher salt

Directions:

1. To prep the "churros": Cut the puff pastry crosswise into 4 rectangles. Fold each piece in half lengthwise to make a long thin "churro."

2. To prep the caramel sauce: Measure the brown sugar, butter, cream, and vanilla into an ovenproof ramekin or bowl (no need to stir).

3. To cook the "churros" and caramel sauce: Install a crisper plate in the Zone 1 basket. Place the "churros" in the basket and insert the basket in the unit. Place the ramekin in the Zone 2 basket and insert the basket in the unit.

4. Select Zone 1, select AIR FRY, set the temperature to 330°F, and set the timer to 10 minutes.

5. Select Zone 2, select BAKE, set the temperature to 350°F, and set the timer to 10 minutes. Select SMART FINISH.

6. Press START/PAUSE to begin cooking.

7. When the Zone 2 timer reads 5 minutes, press START/PAUSE. Remove the basket and stir the caramel. Reinsert the basket and press START/PAUSE to resume cooking.

8. When cooking is complete, the "churros" will be golden brown and cooked through and the caramel sauce smooth.

9. Spritz each "churro" with cooking spray and sprinkle generously with the granulated sugar and cinnamon.

10. Stir the salt into the caramel sauce. Let cool for 5 to 10 minutes before serving. Note that the caramel will thicken as it cools.

Nutrition:

- (Per serving) Calories: 460; Total fat: 26g; Saturated fat: 14g; Carbohydrates: 60g; Fiber: 1.5g; Protein: 5g; Sodium: 254mg

Pumpkin Muffins With Cinnamon

Servings: 4
Cooking Time: 20 Minutes
Ingredients:

- 1 and ½ cups all-purpose flour
- ½ teaspoon baking soda
- ½ teaspoon baking powder
- 1 and ¼ teaspoons cinnamon, groaned
- ¼ teaspoon ground nutmeg, grated
- 2 large eggs
- Salt, pinch
- ¾ cup granulated sugar
- ½ cup dark brown sugar
- 1 and ½ cups pumpkin puree
- ¼ cup coconut milk

Directions:

1. Take 4 ramekins and layer them with muffin paper.
2. In a bowl, add the eggs, brown sugar, baking soda, baking powder, cinnamon, nutmeg, and sugar and whisk well with an electric mixer.
3. In a second bowl, mix the flour, and salt.
4. Slowly add the dry to the wet Ingredients:.
5. Fold in the pumpkin puree and milk and mix it in well.
6. Divide this batter into 4 ramekins.
7. Place two ramekins in each air fryer basket.
8. Set the time for zone 1 to 18 minutes at 360 degrees on AIR FRY mode.
9. Select the MATCH button for the zone 2 basket.
10. Check after the time is up and if not done, and let it AIR FRY for one more minute.
11. Once it is done, serve.

Pumpkin Cookie With Cream Cheese Frosting

Servings: 6
Cooking Time: 7 Minutes
Ingredients:

- 50 g blanched finely ground almond flour
- 50 g powdered sweetener, divided
- 2 tablespoons butter, softened
- 1 large egg
- ½ teaspoon unflavored gelatin
- ½ teaspoon baking powder
- ½ teaspoon vanilla extract
- ½ teaspoon pumpkin pie spice
- 2 tablespoons pure pumpkin purée
- ½ teaspoon ground cinnamon, divided
- 40 g low-carb, sugar-free chocolate chips
- 85 g full-fat cream cheese, softened

Directions:

1. In a large bowl, mix almond flour and 25 gsweetener. Stir in butter, egg, and gelatin until combined. 2. Stir in baking powder, vanilla, pumpkin pie spice, pumpkin purée, and ¼ teaspoon cinnamon, then fold in chocolate chips. 3. Pour batter into a round baking pan. Place pan into the zone 1 air fryer basket. 4. Adjust the temperature to 150ºC and bake for 7 minutes. 5. When fully cooked, the top will be golden brown, and a toothpick inserted in center will come out clean. Let cool at least 20 minutes. 6. To make the frosting: mix cream cheese, remaining ¼ teaspoon cinnamon, and remaining 25 g sweetener in a large bowl. Using an electric mixer, beat until it becomes fluffy. Spread onto the cooled cookie. Garnish with additional cinnamon if desired.

Olive Oil Cake & Old-fashioned Fudge Pie

Servings: 16
Cooking Time: 30 Minutes

Ingredients:

- Olive Oil Cake:
- 120 g blanched finely ground almond flour
- 5 large eggs, whisked
- 175 ml extra-virgin olive oil
- 75 g granulated sweetener
- 1 teaspoon vanilla extract
- 1 teaspoon baking powder
- Old-Fashioned Fudge Pie:
- 300 g granulated sugar
- 40 g unsweetened cocoa powder
- 70 g self-raising flour
- 3 large eggs, unbeaten
- 12 tablespoons unsalted butter, melted
- 1½ teaspoons vanilla extract
- 1 (9-inch) unbaked piecrust
- 30 g icing sugar (optional)

Directions:

1. Make the Olive Oil Cake :
2. In a large bowl, mix all ingredients. Pour batter into an ungreased round nonstick baking dish.
3. Place dish into the zone 1 air fryer basket. Adjust the temperature to 150ºC and bake for 30 minutes. The cake will be golden on top and firm in the center when done.
4. Let cake cool in dish 30 minutes before slicing and serving.
5. Make the Old-Fashioned Fudge Pie :
6. In a medium bowl, stir together the sugar, cocoa powder, and flour. Stir in the eggs and melted butter. Stir in the vanilla.
7. Preheat the air fryer to 175ºC.
8. Pour the chocolate filing into the crust.
9. Cook in the zone 2 basket for 25 to 30 minutes, stirring every 10 minutes, until a knife inserted into the middle comes out clean. Let sit for 5 minutes before dusting with icing sugar to serve.

Apple Hand Pies

Servings: 8

Cooking Time: 21 Minutes.

Ingredients:

- 8 tablespoons butter, softened
- 12 tablespoons brown sugar
- 2 teaspoons cinnamon, ground
- 4 medium Granny Smith apples, diced
- 2 teaspoons cornstarch
- 4 teaspoons cold water
- 1 (14-oz) package pastry, 9-inch crust pie
- Cooking spray
- 1 tablespoon grapeseed oil
- ½ cup powdered sugar
- 2 teaspoons milk

Directions:

1. Toss apples with brown sugar, butter, and cinnamon in a suitable skillet.
2. Place the skillet over medium heat and stir cook for 5 minutes.
3. Mix cornstarch with cold water in a small bowl.
4. Add cornstarch mixture into the apple and cook for 1 minute until it thickens.
5. Remove this filling from the heat and allow it to cool.
6. Unroll the pie crust and spray on a floured surface.
7. Cut the dough into 16 equal rectangles.
8. Wet the edges of the 8 rectangles with water and divide the apple filling at the center of these rectangles.
9. Place the other 8 rectangles on top and crimp the edges with a fork, then make 2-3 slashes on top.
10. Place 4 small pies in each of the crisper plate.
11. Return the crisper plate to the Ninja Foodi Dual Zone Air Fryer.
12. Choose the Air Fry mode for Zone 1 and set the temperature to 390 degrees F and the time to 17 minutes.
13. Select the "MATCH" button to copy the settings for Zone 2.
14. Initiate cooking by pressing the START/STOP button.
15. Flip the pies once cooked halfway through, and resume cooking.
16. Meanwhile, mix sugar with milk.
17. Pour this mixture over the apple pies.
18. Serve fresh.

Nutrition:

- (Per serving) Calories 284 | Fat 16g |Sodium 252mg | Carbs 31.6g | Fiber 0.9g | Sugar 6.6g | Protein 3.7g

Berry Crumble And Coconut-custard Pie

Servings: 8

Cooking Time: 20 To 23 Minutes

Ingredients:

- Berry Crumble:
- For the Filling:
- 300 g mixed berries
- 2 tablespoons sugar
- 1 tablespoon cornflour
- 1 tablespoon fresh lemon juice
- For the Topping:
- 30 g plain flour
- 20 g rolled oats
- 1 tablespoon granulated sugar
- 2 tablespoons cold unsalted butter, cut into small cubes
- Whipped cream or ice cream (optional)
- Coconut-Custard Pie:
- 240 ml milk
- 50 g granulated sugar, plus 2 tablespoons
- 30 g scone mix
- 1 teaspoon vanilla extract
- 2 eggs
- 2 tablespoons melted butter
- Cooking spray
- 50 g desiccated, sweetened coconut

Directions:

1. Make the Berry Crumble :
2. 1. Preheat the air fryer to 205°C. For the filling: In a round baking pan, gently mix the berries, sugar, cornflour, and lemon juice until thoroughly combined. 3. For the topping: In a small bowl, combine the flour, oats, and sugar. Stir the butter into the flour mixture until the mixture has the consistency of breadcrumbs. 4. Sprinkle the topping over the berries. 5. Put the pan in the zone 1 air fryer basket and air fry for 15 minutes. Let cool for 5 minutes on a wire rack. 6. Serve topped with whipped cream or ice cream, if desired.
3. Make the Coconut-Custard Pie :
4. Place all ingredients except coconut in a medium bowl.
5. Using a hand mixer, beat on high speed for 3 minutes.
6. Let sit for 5 minutes.
7. Preheat the air fryer to 165°C.
8. Spray a baking pan with cooking spray and place pan in the zone 2 air fryer basket.
9. Pour filling into pan and sprinkle coconut over top.
10. Cook pie for 20 to 23 minutes or until center sets.

Fried Oreos

Servings: 8
Cooking Time: 8 Minutes
Ingredients:

- 1 can Pillsbury Crescent Dough (or equivalent)
- 8 Oreo cookies
- 1–2 tablespoons powdered sugar

Directions:

1. Open the crescent dough up and cut it into the right-size pieces to completely wrap each cookie.
2. Wrap each Oreo in dough. Make sure that there are no air bubbles and that the cookies are completely covered.
3. Install a crisper plate in both drawers. Place half the Oreo cookies in the zone 1 drawer and half in zone 2's. Sprinkle the tops with the powdered sugar, then insert the drawers into the unit.
4. Select zone 1, select AIR FRY, set temperature to 390°F, and set time to 8 minutes. Select MATCH to match zone 2 settings to zone 1. Press the START/STOP button to begin cooking.
5. Serve warm and enjoy!

Gluten-free Spice Cookies

Servings: 4
Cooking Time: 12 Minutes
Ingredients:

- 4 tablespoons unsalted butter, at room temperature
- 2 tablespoons agave nectar
- 1 large egg
- 2 tablespoons water
- 240 g almond flour
- 100 g granulated sugar
- 2 teaspoons ground ginger
- 1 teaspoon ground cinnamon
- ½ teaspoon freshly grated nutmeg
- 1 teaspoon baking soda
- ¼ teaspoon kosher, or coarse sea salt

Directions:

1. Line the bottom of the air fryer basket with baking paper cut to fit.
2. In a large bowl, using a hand mixer, beat together the butter, agave, egg, and water on medium speed until light and fluffy.
3. Add the almond flour, sugar, ginger, cinnamon, nutmeg, baking soda, and salt. Beat on low speed until well combined.
4. Roll the dough into 2-tablespoon balls and arrange them on the baking paper in the basket. Set the air fryer to 165°C, and cook for 12 minutes, or until the tops of cookies are lightly browned.
5. Transfer to a wire rack and let cool completely. Store in an airtight container for up to a week.

Pumpkin Hand Pies Blueberry Hand Pies

Servings:4

Cooking Time: 15 Minutes

Ingredients:

- FOR THE PUMPKIN HAND PIES
- ½ cup pumpkin pie filling (from a 15-ounce can)
- ⅓ cup half-and-half
- 1 large egg
- ¼ cup blueberries
- 2 tablespoons granulated sugar
- 1 tablespoon grated lemon zest (optional)
- ¼ teaspoon cornstarch
- 1 teaspoon fresh lemon juice
- ⅛ teaspoon kosher salt
- ½ refrigerated pie crust (from a 14.1-ounce package)
- 1 large egg yolk
- 1 tablespoon whole milk
- ½ teaspoon turbinado sugar
- ½ refrigerated pie crust (from a 14.1-ounce package)
- 1 large egg yolk
- 1 tablespoon whole milk
- FOR THE BLUEBERRY HAND PIES

Directions:

1. To prep the pumpkin hand pies: In a small bowl, mix the pumpkin pie filling, half-and-half, and whole egg until well combined and smooth.

2. Cut the dough in half to form two wedges. Divide the pumpkin pie filling between the wedges. Fold the crust over to completely encase the filling. Using a fork, crimp the edges, forming a tight seal.

3. In a small bowl, whisk together the egg yolk and milk. Brush over the pastry. Carefully cut two small vents in the top of each pie.

4. To prep the blueberry hand pies: In a small bowl, combine the blueberries, granulated sugar, lemon zest (if using), cornstarch, lemon juice, and salt.

5. Cut the dough in half to form two wedges. Divide the blueberry filling between the wedges. Fold the crust over to completely encase the filling. Using a fork, crimp the edges, forming a tight seal.

6. In a small bowl, whisk together the egg yolk and milk. Brush over the pastry. Sprinkle with the turbinado sugar. Carefully cut two small vents in the top of each pie.

7. To cook the hand pies: Install a crisper plate in each of the two baskets. Place the pumpkin hand pies in the Zone 1 basket and insert the basket in the unit. Place the blueberry hand pies in the Zone 2 basket and insert the basket in the unit.

8. Select Zone 1, select AIR FRY, set the temperature to 350°F, and set the timer to 15 minutes. Select MATCH COOK to match Zone 2 settings to Zone 1.

9. Press START/PAUSE to begin cooking.

10. When cooking is complete, the pie crust should be crisp and golden brown and the filling bubbling.

11. Let the hand pies cool for at least 30 minutes before serving.

Nutrition:

- (Per serving) Calories: 588; Total fat: 33g; Saturated fat: 14g; Carbohydrates: 68g; Fiber: 0.5g; Protein: 10g; Sodium: 583mg

Dessert Empanadas

Servings: 12

Cooking Time: 10 Minutes

Ingredients:

- 12 empanada wrappers thawed
- 2 apples, chopped
- 2 tablespoons raw honey
- 1 teaspoon vanilla extract
- 1 teaspoon cinnamon
- ⅛ teaspoon nutmeg
- 2 teaspoons cornstarch
- 1 teaspoon water
- 1 egg beaten

Directions:

1. Mix apples with vanilla, honey, nutmeg, and cinnamon in a saucepan.
2. Cook for 3 minutes then mix cornstarch with water and pour into the pan.
3. Cook for 30 seconds.
4. Allow this filling to cool and keep it aside.
5. Spread the wrappers on the working surface.
6. Divide the apple filling on top of the wrappers.
7. Fold the wrappers in half and seal the edges by pressing them.
8. Brush the empanadas with the beaten egg and place them in the air fryer basket 1.
9. Return the air fryer basket 1 to Zone 1 of the Ninja Foodi 2-Basket Air Fryer.
10. Choose the "Air Fry" mode for Zone 1 at 400 degrees F and 10 minutes of cooking time.
11. Initiate cooking by pressing the START/PAUSE BUTTON.
12. Flip the empanadas once cooked halfway through.
13. Serve.

Nutrition:

- (Per serving) Calories 204 | Fat 9g |Sodium 91mg | Carbs 27g | Fiber 2.4g | Sugar 15g | Protein 1.3g

Berry Crumble And S'mores

Servings: 8
Cooking Time: 15 Minutes

Ingredients:

- Berry Crumble:
- For the Filling:
- 300 g mixed berries
- 2 tablespoons sugar
- 1 tablespoon cornflour
- 1 tablespoon fresh lemon juice
- For the Topping:
- 30 g plain flour
- 20 g rolled oats
- 1 tablespoon granulated sugar
- 2 tablespoons cold unsalted butter, cut into small cubes
- Whipped cream or ice cream (optional)
- S'mores:
- Coconut, or avocado oil, for spraying
- 8 digestive biscuits
- 2 (45 g) chocolate bars
- 4 large marshmallows

Directions:

1. Make the Berry Crumble :
2. 1. Preheat the air fryer to 204°C. For the filling: In a round baking pan, gently mix the berries, sugar, cornflour, and lemon juice until thoroughly combined. 3. For the topping: In a small bowl, combine the flour, oats, and sugar. Stir the butter into the flour mixture until the mixture has the consistency of breadcrumbs. 4. Sprinkle the topping over the berries. 5. Put the pan in the zone 1 air fryer drawer and air fry for 15 minutes. Let cool for 5 minutes on a wire rack. 6. Serve topped with whipped cream or ice cream, if desired.
3. Make the S'mores :
4. Line the zone 2 air fryer drawer with baking paper and spray lightly with oil.
5. Place 4 biscuits into the prepared drawer.
6. Break the chocolate bars in half, and place 1/2 on top of each biscuit. Top with 1 marshmallow.
7. Air fry at 188°C for 30 seconds, or until the marshmallows are puffed, golden brown and slightly melted.
8. Top with the remaining biscuits and serve.

Butter Cake

Servings: 6
Cooking Time: 20 Minutes

Ingredients:

- 1 egg
- 3 tablespoons butter, softened
- ½ cup milk
- 1 tablespoon icing sugar
- ½ cup caster sugar
- 1½ cup plain flour
- A pinch of salt

Directions:

1. In a bowl, add the butter and sugar. Whisk until creamy.
2. Now, add the egg and whisk until fluffy.
3. Add the flour and salt. Mix well with the milk.
4. Place the mixture evenly into the greased cake pan.
5. Press "Zone 1" and "Zone 2" and then rotate the knob for each zone to select "Air Fry".
6. Set the temperature to 350 degrees F/ 175 degrees C for both zones and then set the time for 5 minutes to preheat.
7. After preheating, arrange the pan into the basket of each zone.
8. Slide each basket into Air Fryer and set the time for 15 minutes.
9. After cooking time is completed, remove the pan from Air Fryer.
10. Set aside to cool.
11. Serve and enjoy!

Walnut Baklava Bites Pistachio Baklava Bites

Servings:12

Cooking Time: 10 Minutes

Ingredients:

- FOR THE WALNUT BAKLAVA BITES
- ¼ cup finely chopped walnuts
- 2 teaspoons cold unsalted butter, grated
- 2 teaspoons granulated sugar
- ½ teaspoon ground cinnamon
- 6 frozen phyllo shells (from a 1.9-ounce package), thawed
- FOR THE PISTACHIO BAKLAVA BITES
- ¼ cup finely chopped pistachios
- 2 teaspoons very cold unsalted butter, grated
- 2 teaspoons granulated sugar
- ¼ teaspoon ground cardamom (optional)
- 6 frozen phyllo shells (from a 1.9-ounce package), thawcd
- FOR THE HONEY SYRUP
- ¼ cup hot water
- ¼ cup honey
- 2 teaspoons fresh lemon juice

Directions:

1. To prep the walnut baklava bites: In a small bowl, combine the walnuts, butter, sugar, and cinnamon. Spoon the filling into the phyllo shells.

2. To prep the pistachio baklava bites: In a small bowl, combine the pistachios, butter, sugar, and cardamom (if using). Spoon the filling into the phyllo shells.

3. To cook the baklava bites: Install a crisper plate in each of the two baskets. Place the walnut baklava bites in the Zone 1 basket and insert the basket in the unit. Place the pistachio baklava bites in the Zone 2 basket and insert the basket in the unit.

4. Select Zone 1, select BAKE, set the temperature to 330°F, and set the timer to 10 minutes. Press MATCH COOK to match Zone 2 settings to Zone 1.

5. Press START/PAUSE to begin cooking.

6. When cooking is complete, the shells will be golden brown and crisp.

7. To make the honey syrup: In a small bowl, whisk together the hot water, honey, and lemon juice. Dividing evenly, pour the syrup over the baklava bites (you may hear a crackling sound).

8. Let cool completely before serving, about 1 hour.

Nutrition:

- (Per serving) Calories: 262; Total fat: 16g; Saturated fat: 3g; Carbohydrates: 29g; Fiber: 1g; Protein: 2g; Sodium: 39mg

Chocolate Pudding

Servings: 2
Cooking Time: 12 Minutes
Ingredients:

- 1 egg
- 32g all-purpose flour
- 35g cocoa powder
- 50g sugar
- 57g butter, melted
- ½ tsp baking powder

Directions:

1. In a bowl, mix flour, cocoa powder, sugar, and baking powder.
2. Add egg and butter and stir until well combined.
3. Pour batter into the two greased ramekins.
4. Insert a crisper plate in Ninja Foodi air fryer baskets.
5. Place ramekins in both baskets.
6. Select zone 1 then select "bake" mode and set the temperature to 375 degrees F for 12 minutes. Press match cook to match zone 2 settings to zone 1. Press "start/stop" to begin.

Nutrition:

- (Per serving) Calories 512 | Fat 27.3g |Sodium 198mg | Carbs 70.6g | Fiber 4.7g | Sugar 50.5g | Protein 7.2g

Jelly Donuts

Servings: 4
Cooking Time: 5 Minutes
Ingredients:

- 1 package Pillsbury Grands (Homestyle)
- ½ cup seedless raspberry jelly
- 1 tablespoon butter, melted
- ½ cup sugar

Directions:

1. Install a crisper plate in both drawers. Place half of the biscuits in the zone 1 drawer and half in zone 2's, then insert the drawers into the unit. You may need to cook in batches.
2. Select zone 1, select AIR FRY, set temperature to 390°F, and set time to 22 minutes. Select MATCH to match zone 2 settings to zone 1. Press the START/STOP button to begin cooking.
3. Place the sugar into a wide bowl with a flat bottom.
4. Baste all sides of the cooked biscuits with the melted butter and roll in the sugar to cover completely.
5. Using a long cake tip, pipe 1–2 tablespoons of raspberry jelly into each biscuit. You've now got raspberry-filled donuts!

Spiced Apple Cake

Servings: 6
Cooking Time: 30 Minutes
Ingredients:

- Vegetable oil
- 2 diced & peeled Gala apples
- 1 tablespoon fresh lemon juice
- 55 g unsalted butter, softened
- 65 g granulated sugar
- 2 large eggs
- 155 g plain flour
- 1½ teaspoons baking powder
- 1 tablespoon apple pie spice
- ½ teaspoon ground ginger
- ¼ teaspoon ground cardamom
- ¼ teaspoon ground nutmeg
- ½ teaspoon kosher, or coarse sea salt
- 60 ml whole milk
- Icing sugar, for dusting

Directions:

1. Grease a 0.7-liter Bundt, or tube pan with oil; set aside.
2. In a medium bowl, toss the apples with the lemon juice until well coated; set aside.
3. In a large bowl, combine the butter and sugar. Beat with an electric hand mixer on medium speed until the sugar has dissolved. Add the eggs and beat until fluffy. Add the flour, baking powder, apple pie spice, ginger, cardamom, nutmeg, salt, and milk. Mix until the batter is thick but pourable.
4. Pour the batter into the prepared pan. Top batter evenly with the apple mixture. Place the pan in the zone 1 air fryer drawer. Set the temperature to 176°C and cook for 30 minutes, or until a toothpick inserted in the center of the cake comes out clean. Close the air fryer and let the cake rest for 10 minutes. Turn the cake out onto a wire rack and cool completely.
5. Right before serving, dust the cake with icing sugar.

Dehydrated Peaches

Servings: 4
Cooking Time: 8 Hours
Ingredients:

- 300g canned peaches

Directions:

1. Insert a crisper plate in the Ninja Foodi air fryer baskets.
2. Place peaches in both baskets.
3. Select zone 1, then select "dehydrate" mode and set the temperature to 135 degrees F for 8 hours. Press "start/stop" to begin.

Nutrition:

- (Per serving) Calories 30 | Fat 0.2g |Sodium 0mg | Carbs 7g | Fiber 1.2g | Sugar 7g | Protein 0.7g

Mocha Pudding Cake Vanilla Pudding Cake

Servings:8

Cooking Time: 25 Minutes

Ingredients:

- FOR THE MOCHA PUDDING CAKE
- 1 cup all-purpose flour
- ⅔ cup granulated sugar
- 1 cup packed light brown sugar, divided
- 5 tablespoons unsweetened cocoa powder, divided
- 2 teaspoons baking powder
- ¼ teaspoon kosher salt
- ½ cup unsweetened almond milk
- 2 teaspoons vanilla extract
- 2 tablespoons vegetable oil
- 1 cup freshly brewed coffee
- FOR THE VANILLA PUDDING CAKE
- 1 cup all-purpose flour
- ⅔ cup granulated sugar, plus ½ cup
- 2 teaspoons baking powder
- ¼ teaspoon kosher salt
- ½ cup unsweetened almond milk
- 2½ teaspoons vanilla extract, divided
- 2 tablespoons vegetable oil
- ¾ cup hot water
- 2 teaspoons cornstarch

Directions:

1. To prep the mocha pudding cake: In a medium bowl, combine the flour, granulated sugar, ½ cup of brown sugar, 3 tablespoons of cocoa powder, the baking powder, and salt. Stir in the almond milk, vanilla, and oil to form a thick batter.
2. Spread the batter in the bottom of the Zone 1 basket. Sprinkle the remaining ½ cup brown sugar and 2 tablespoons of cocoa powder in an even layer over the batter. Gently pour the hot coffee over the batter (do not mix).
3. To prep the vanilla pudding cake: In a medium bowl, combine the flour, ⅔ cup of granulated sugar, the baking powder, and salt. Stir in the almond milk, 2 teaspoons of vanilla, and the oil to form a thick batter.
4. Spread the batter in the bottom of the Zone 2 basket.
5. In a small bowl, whisk together the hot water, cornstarch, and remaining ½ cup of sugar and ½ teaspoon of vanilla. Gently pour over the batter (do not mix).
6. To cook both pudding cakes: Insert both baskets in the unit.
7. Select Zone 1, select BAKE, set the temperature to 330°F, and set the timer to 25 minutes. Select MATCH COOK to match Zone 2 settings to Zone 1.
8. Press START/PAUSE to begin cooking.
9. When cooking is complete, the tops of the cakes should be dry and set.
10. Let the cakes rest for 10 minutes before serving. The pudding will thicken as it cools.

Nutrition:

- (Per serving) Calories: 531; Total fat: 8g; Saturated fat: 1g; Carbohydrates: 115g; Fiber: 3.5g; Protein: 5g; Sodium: 111mg

Lemon Sugar Cookie Bars Monster Sugar Cookie Bars

Servings:12

Cooking Time: 18 Minutes

Ingredients:

- FOR THE LEMON COOKIE BARS
- Grated zest and juice of 1 lemon
- ½ cup granulated sugar
- 4 tablespoons (½ stick) unsalted butter, at room temperature
- 1 large egg yolk
- 1 teaspoon vanilla extract
- ⅛ teaspoon baking powder
- ½ cup plus 2 tablespoons all-purpose flour
- FOR THE MONSTER COOKIE BARS
- ½ cup granulated sugar
- 4 tablespoons (½ stick) unsalted butter, at room temperature
- 1 large egg yolk
- 1 teaspoon vanilla extract
- ⅛ teaspoon baking powder
- ½ cup plus 2 tablespoons all-purpose flour
- ¼ cup rolled oats
- ¼ cup M&M's
- ¼ cup peanut butter chips

Directions:

1. To prep the lemon cookie bars: In a large bowl, rub together the lemon zest and sugar. Add the butter and use a hand mixer to beat until light and fluffy.

2. Beat in the egg yolk, vanilla, and lemon juice. Mix in the baking powder and flour.

3. To prep the monster cookie bars: In a large bowl, with a hand mixer, beat the sugar and butter until light and fluffy.

4. Beat in the egg yolk and vanilla. Mix in the baking powder and flour. Stir in the oats, M&M's, and peanut butter chips.

5. To cook the cookie bars: Line both baskets with aluminum foil. Press the lemon cookie dough into the Zone 1 basket and insert the basket in the unit. Press the monster cookie dough into the Zone 2 basket and insert the basket in the unit.

6. Select Zone 1, select BAKE, set the temperature to 330°F, and set the timer to 18 minutes. Press MATCH COOK to match Zone 2 settings to Zone 1.

7. Press START/PAUSE to begin cooking.

8. When cooking is complete, the cookies should be set in the middle and have begun to pull away from the sides of the basket.

9. Let the cookies cool completely, about 1 hour. Cut each basket into 6 bars for a total of 12 bars.

Nutrition:

- (Per serving) Calories: 191; Total fat: 8.5g; Saturated fat: 5g; Carbohydrates: 27g; Fiber: 0.5g; Protein: 2g; Sodium: 3mg

Recipe Index

Printed in Great Britain
by Amazon

40689045R00059